chinese
horoscopes
 for beginners

chinese horoscopes
for beginners

KRISTYNA ARCARTI

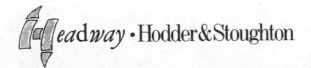

Headway · Hodder & Stoughton

Cataloguing in Publication Data is available from the British Library

ISBN 0 340 64804 X

First published 1995
Impression number   10 9 8 7 6 5 4 3 2 1
Year   1999 1998 1997 1996 1995

Typeset by Transet Limited, Coventry, England
Printed in Great Britain for Hodder & Stoughton Educational, a division of Hodder Headline plc, 338 Euston Road, London NW1 3BH by Cox & Wyman Ltd, Reading, Berkshire.

For Beginners

This series of books is written for the growing number of people who, disillusioned with the sterility of our technological age, are looking to traditional, esoteric arts to find out more about themselves and others.

Other books in the series include:

Tarot for Beginners
Star Signs for Beginners
Palmistry for Beginners
Numerology for Beginners
Gems and Crystals for Beginners
Graphology for Beginners
Dowsing for Beginners
Feng Shui for Beginners
Chakras for Beginners
I Ching for Beginners
Love Signs for Beginners
Meditation for Beginners
Visualisation for Beginners

To John's Mandarin friend, who has been with me throughout the writing of this book. Many thanks.

CONTENTS

Chapter 4   The years   91

Chapter 5   Compatibility   111

Further reading   117

INTRODUCTION

In China, astrology is more than a pastime; it is an important part of daily life. In fact, lists of stars and maps of the heavens existed in China long before there was anything of that kind in the Western world.

Most people are aware of the Western zodiac, and many read 'the stars' in the paper each day. However, few are equally familiar with Chinese astrology, which also offers information on your character traits and likely future.

The Western and oriental forms of astrology are not the only ones. The oldest is often said to be the Hindu system. This can be a very complicated form, looking at the whole lifetime of the subject under discussion rather than just at the date and time of birth. The Chinese or oriental system is much easier to understand.

It should be noted that no single system of astrology is more correct than the others. They complement each other, and many authorities have studied more than one, and to great effect.

Fundamental to Chinese astrology is the concept of yin and yang, complementary opposites. This is echoed in Western astrology by the polarities, positive and negative, and there are other similarities in the two systems.

Chinese astrology, like Western astrology has twelve zodiac signs, but whereas Western zodiac signs last for approximately a month, Chinese signs last for a year. They do not run from January to December but are based on lunar months. Thus the New Year begins

on a different date each year. Each of the years is assigned its own animal emblem. Each animal has its own personal characteristics, in much the same way as each Western zodiac sign has its own set of individual traits.

Another similarity is that in the Chinese system, as in the Western, compatibilities can be made between one sign and another. In addition, each is subdivided into five elements – earth, fire, wood, metal and water. Those who know a little about the Western zodiac will know that each star sign also has an element associated with it, in this case the four elements of earth, air, fire and water. In Chinese astrology each animal has all five elements attached to it. However, more of that later.

The aim behind this book is to give the beginner information from which to move forward. As with any form of astrology, there is more to it than basic character interpretation. Full Chinese horoscopes take into account not only the year of birth but, as with the Western system, also the month, day and time.

The Chinese system can be linked to the I Ching, the subject of another book in this series, providing information on lucky periods. Further work can be done using what are known as the Four Pillars, the Five Elements and the lifecycle chart. This will be left to later study. The emphasis here will be on discovering which animal signs apply to which years, learning more about the 12 animals which make up the Chinese system, and using our knowledge to forecast general trends and assess personal compatibility.

In the course of reading this book you will learn more about yourself and your compatibility with others. However, you must keep an open mind. With any form of astrology, whether oriental or Western, or indeed using any esoteric help, you must retain personal responsibility. Different backgrounds, circumstances, beliefs and faiths make us all individuals. No two people are totally alike.

Chinese astrology does not emphasise prediction although it identifies trends. It is more character-oriented than its Western counterpart, giving us pathways of thought rather than direct routes towards a future goal.

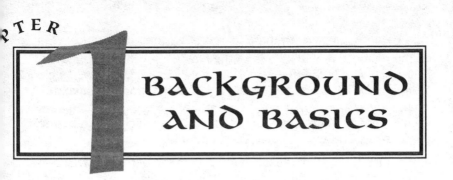

BACKGROUND AND BASICS

This chapter looks at the history of Chinese astrology. It explains the origins of the 12 animal signs and gives their years. It also introduces the Chinese calendar and system of time-keeping. Finally it explains the importance of the Five Elements and the concept of yin and yang.

History

As with many forms of self-help and self-awareness, the actual date of origin of Chinese horoscopes is not known. It has been placed variously between 4000 and 2000 BC. What is certain, however, is that the Chinese have been practising astrology for many thousands of years. Astrology in China was at its height around the time of the Middle Ages.

Astrology was especially popular in China around the time of the Emperor Fu Hsi, between 2953 and 2838 BC, and it continued to evolve from that time. The emperor was considered to be the high priest of the heavens, and made sacrifices to the stars in order to remain in harmony with them. The four corners of the emperor's palace represented the cardinal points in space, located by the equinoxes and solstices, and he and his family are said to have moved from one corner to another, as the seasons changed.

Chinese legend suggests that more than five centuries before the birth of Christ, when Chinese astrology was already well established, the dying Buddha asked all the animals of the world to come before

him to bid them farewell, for which they would receive gifts. Many of the animals, probably fearing the reasoning behind the request, failed to arrive before the Buddha. Those who did, however, were 12 in number. They were the rat, ox, tiger, rabbit, dragon, snake, horse, goat, monkey, rooster, dog and pig. To thank these animals for coming, the Buddha offered each one a year, which would be theirs for all time. This would make each animal immortal.

Each animal year would start with the advent of the Chinese New Year which is based on the lunar cycle. Each year was then given an animal name and ascribed the traits of that animal, and thus everyone born in that year acquired the personality and behaviour patterns associated with the animal. A cycle of 12 years was then established. In addition, the day was broken down into two-hour periods and given animals, and the months of the year were similarly designated – but more of that later.

It might be worthwhile pointing out at this stage that the Vietnamese, Tibetan, Japanese and Korean animal names are often slightly different from the Chinese. The rabbit becomes the cat, and the pig becomes the wild boar. Yet again some use the sheep instead of the goat, the buffalo or bull instead of the ox, and the mouse instead of the rat. In this book we are going to follow the conventional 12 Chinese animal signs.

History tells us that when China became an empire, anyone seen to be practising astrology could be condemned to death, despite the reverence in which it was held. This was because the secrets of the stars were considered to belong solely in the hands of the Emperor, as were secrets of state. In fact the Emperor had his own Grand Astrologer, as is noted in the court documents of the second century BC, and it was considered a debasement for the astrologer to cast the horoscope of a mere commoner.

It is said that when the Dowager Empress Tzu'hi died, the timing of her funeral was worked out by the court astrologers, as it had been for all the rulers of the Celestial Empire.

The work of court astrologers in tracking the motions of the planets, and stars is still used by astronomers today.

The earlier forms of Chinese astrology, promulgated mainly by the Buddhist monks, used a system of 12 branches, and the first mention of the animals to which we have referred seems to occur around the eighth or ninth century. It was definitely in popular use in AD 10. The use of this form then increased in popularity and was seen in many Asian countries. One theory suggests that, as seven of the animals attributed to the eight trigrams in the I Ching or Chinese Book of Changes relate to the animals in Chinese astrology, their adoption into the system came about because of the I Ching. Another suggestion is that considerable consultation took place about which animal was given which year, and that meteorological and agricultural data was considered, the Chinese being particularly fond of working to seasonal changes.

Some say that the rat became the first emblem or sign because the rat represented midnight on Chinese clocks, the start of a new day, rather than, as legend would have us believe, because the rat was the first animal to appear before the Buddha. In some stories, the rat rounded up the other animals, and nearly got missed out when the Buddha was making his choice. To make himself visible, it is said, he stood on the back of another animal.

On taking a closer look at the animals which make up the 12 Chinese emblems, it becomes clear that they divide neatly into two groups of six animals, one group active, the other passive. This is the yin/yang element which we will discuss shortly.

A full Chinese horoscope chart takes into account many factors, including the 28 lunar mansions, or *Hsiu*, the length of the solar year, the stars, 10 heavenly stems, the previously mentioned 12 earthly branches which were for the most part taken over by the 12 animal signs, the four pillars, the lodges, and the times and dates of the solstices and equinoxes. A full discussion of these factors is beyond the scope of this book. However, it is worth understanding, even for the beginner, that the four pillars are the time, day, month and year of birth, and each of these pillars has a stem and a branch, giving eight characters in all, linking with the eight trigrams of the I Ching.

In some cases, the 10 stems have been overtaken by the five elements, which we will discuss shortly.

It is also worth noting that the ancient Chinese counted the days in tens, making a sort of 10-day week, known as *Hsun*. This is the origin of the 10 heavenly stems. Later, years were reckoned in 12s, according to the position of the planet Jupiter, whose orbital motion takes approximately 12 years. These became the 12 branches, referred to above. In fact, China's old calendar began in the year 2736 BC, during the reign of Emperor Nuang-ti. This emperor is credited with the discovery of the sexennial cycle of the planet Jupiter, which is the basic key to Chinese astrological calculations.

Those who wish to study oriental astrology further should be aware of the fact that the constellations are different from the Western ones, not only in name, but in the way in which the stars are grouped. Only 10 have any similarity with the Western system. Similarly, the division of times, seasons and dates is different. The day is divided into 12 double hours or *Chih*, each with its own symbol and name. It was not until around AD 220 that they were linked with the names of the animals.

Chinese horoscopes at work

As we have seen, the Chinese system is based on 12 animals, each with its own year. This starts sometime between the end of January and early February, the actual date varying from year to year,

In this multi cultural society in which we live, many Western people will be aware of the celebrations heralding the Chinese New Year, when colourful processions led by the mythical Dragon sweep the street, and banquets abound. Most, however, will be unaware of the fact that the timing is based on the lunar cycle, like the rest of the Chinese calendar. Owing to this fact, those born in January or February of any year should refer to the precise dates of Chinese years given below each animal section as we discuss it later. Likewise, those born close to the start or end of a Chinese year should bear in mind that they may also be subject to influences from the other animal year.

The Animal Years

Rat	1900	1912	1924	1936	1948	1960	1972	1984	1996
Ox	1901	1913	1925	1937	1949	1961	1973	1985	1997
Tiger	1902	1914	1926	1938	1950	1962	1974	1986	1998
Rabbit	1903	1915	1927	1939	1951	1963	1975	1987	1999
Dragon	1904	1916	1928	1940	1952	1964	1976	1988	2000
Snake	1905	1917	1929	1941	1953	1965	1977	1989	2001
Horse	1906	1918	1930	1942	1954	1966	1978	1990	2002
Goat	1907	1919	1931	1943	1955	1967	1979	1991	2003
Monkey	1908	1920	1932	1944	1956	1968	1980	1992	2004
Rooster	1909	1921	1933	1945	1957	1969	1981	1993	2005
Dog	1910	1922	1934	1946	1958	1970	1982	1994	2006
Pig	1911	1923	1935	1947	1959	1971	1983	1995	2007

Months and double hours

As we have already mentioned, in addition to the animals being given a year, each month and two-hour period, or 'double hour', is assigned an animal. These are as follows:

Sign	Month	Time
Rat	December	11pm – 1am
Ox	January	1am – 3am
Tiger	February	3am – 5am
Rabbit	March	5am – 7am
Dragon	April	7am – 9am
Snake	May	9am – 11am
Horse	June	11am – 1pm
Goat	July	1pm – 3pm
Monkey	August	3pm – 5pm
Rooster	September	5pm – 7pm
Dog	October	7pm – 9pm
Pig	November	9pm – 11pm

It is worth noting here that the ancient Chinese day began at 11pm, not at midnight, hence the first of the 12 two-hour periods started at 11pm. It is said that the positive (yang) forces of the universe were beginning to return at that time.

Lucky and unlucky years

The Chinese believe that people born in the year of a particular animal have certain personal characteristics peculiar to that year. As a result, for each sign, some years will be more favourable than others. An easy way to show this is to place the 12 animal signs around a clockface.

Animals at 120 degree angles are favourable to each other, while those at 90 degree or 180 degree are unfavourable. Therefore, for someone born in the year of the rat, dragon and monkey years are fortunate, but rabbit, horse and rooster years are not.

This also applies to compatibility between those born in certain years. Harmonious relationships can be made with those people born in the 30 degree angle years, midway between the fortunate years. As a result, rats can be friendly with monkeys and tigers, but tigers and monkeys will not get on well, because they are in direct opposition to each other.

The elements

Another aspect of Chinese astrology is its concept of the five elements, whose first use is historically attributed to the philosopher Chou Yen. These elements are the agents which create change. In Western astrology there are four elements: earth, air, fire and water. In the Chinese system there are five: wood, fire, earth, metal and water, in that order. This sequence is known as the productive order, because wood burns, producing fire, which leaves behind earth (ash) which is mined to extract metal, which when smelted flows like water, which in turn nourishes the trees (wood), and so on in a cycle.

Interestingly, if you choose to look at alternating elements, you will discover a destructive element, as wood (trees and plants) takes nourishment from the earth, earth clouds water, water puts out fire, fire melts metal and metal chops wood.

It is no wonder that the Chinese system considers that two people are likely to get on well with each other if their elements are neighbouring, whereas if they fall in the alternating sequence, the likelihood of a happy relationship is lessened, unless someone whose element falls between the two can act as mediator.

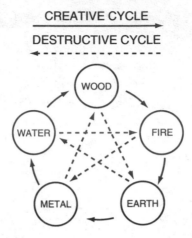

CREATIVE CYCLE

DESTRUCTIVE CYCLE

It is also worth considering how this relates to people, in that a metal person might conquer a wood person by aggression or force, either mental or physical, whereas the wood person might weaken the earth person financially or emotionally. Likewise the earth person may sully the reputation of the water person, whilst of course, fire and water are not compatible at all, as water puts out fire, or at least reduces it to steam!

It is also worth noting that the element of the season in which someone is born may be more important in determining their fate than the element of their birth year. Someone born in spring (February – April) has wood as their element, early summer is fire, late summer is earth, autumn (October – November) is metal, and winter is water.

The number five is, incidentally, very important in China (students of numerology please note). There are not only five planets, but, as we know, five elements, as well as five cardinal points, five governing Lords for cardinal points, five senses and five internal organs.

The five elements correspond to the planets known to the ancient Chinese – Wood being Jupiter, Fire being Mars, Earth being Saturn, Metal being Venus and Water being Mercury. Those familiar with Western astrology will be struck by the connections between fire and Mars, earth and Saturn. In Western astrology the fire sign Aries is ruled by Mars, and the earth sign Capricorn by Saturn.

Planet	Jupiter	Mars	Saturn	Venus	Mercury
Element	Wood	Fire	Earth	Metal	Water
Cardinal point	East	South	Middle	West	North
Governing Lord	Green Dragon	Red Bird	Yellow Emperor	White Tiger	Black Warrior
Sense	Smell	Sight	Touch	Taste	Hearing
Internal organ	Spleen	Lungs	Heart	Liver	Kidneys
Season	Spring	Summer	Late summer	Autumn	Winter
Emotion	Rage/ altruism	Passion	Worry	Nostalgia	Sympathy

The elements also link to various health problems, irrespective of the five internal organs mentioned above:

Wood Liver, gallbladder and digestive problems

Fire Small intestine

Earth Pancreas and mouth

Metal Lungs, respiratory system, large intestine

Water Bladder, ear infections

Those readers who wonder why air does not feature in the elements might like to know that, to the Chinese, air or *Chi* (sometimes seen as *qi*) is considered the life force itself, and so is not represented in this system. Students of Taoism and of yoga, as well as other Eastern systems, will already have met this seeming anomaly.

The ancient Chinese considered that the planets influenced not only mankind, but also nature. Hence connections were perceived such as that between water, which is fluid and swift, and the planet Mercury, which relates to communication and travel. Likewise, Saturn, slow-moving and stable, was easily linked with earth, and Jupiter with wood and therefore with growth and development, and so on.

There are further associations with the five elements:

wood

Family, health, marriage, creativity. High standards but quite expansive. Loyal and fair. Rustic and casual person. Profession: agriculture or medicine. Colour: green. Animal: tiger. Lesser yang.

fire

Temperature, intellect and animals. Dynamism, self-motivation and passion. Often lacking in self-control. Restless or competitive person. Profession: science or industry. Colour: red. Animals: rabbit and dog. Greater yang.

earth

Property, buildings. Dependable and methodical. Down to earth and practical, looks to preserve the past and present for the future. Reliable, conservative person. Profession: mining or construction. Colour: yellow. Animals: rat and ox. Balance.

metal

Trade and military activity. Resilient, competitive, unbending and strong. Independence is important. Eloquent and progressive person. Profession: law or something creative. Colour: white. Animals: dragon and rooster. Lesser yin.

water

Communication, travel, writing skills and artistic pursuits. Sympathetic, tactful and kind. Thoughtful, persistent and profound person. Profession: administration or teaching. Colour: black. Animals: snake, monkey and pig. Greater yin.

You may notice that the horse and goat are not included here. That is because they traditionally relate to planets other than those mentioned above and do not have an element. The horse relates to the Sun and the goat to the Moon. Both sun and moon have a place within the

Chinese system, the sun being yang, and the moon being yin.

Chinese horoscopes are concerned with five possible events, which correspond in some way to the five elements. These possible five forces are fate, seal, wealth, opportunity and official, all of which occur at some time in a person's lifetime. These forces, however, depend on the particular element in play at the time. Again this is better left to future study.

Each year, as a different animal emblem comes into play, so also does a different element. For example, in the year 1971 (the year of the Pig), the element was metal. After we have discussed each animal of the Chinese system, we will look at these elements and the effects each has on the basic character of each animal type.

It is worth noting that the five cardinal points (north, south, east, west and centre), were used at least a thousand years before their use in the West, and these too have a strong connection with the eight main trigrams of the I Ching, which also have links relating to family, the seasons, the elements, the directions and animals, as well as polarities. Those readers who wish to increase their knowledge of Chinese astrology will find that the I Ching and the eight trigrams on which it is based are very important in the full interpretation of Chinese astrology.

YIN AND YANG

In addition to all this new information necessary for an initial understanding of Chinese horoscopes, we must also discuss the yin and yang connection.

Yin and yang, feminine and masculine, are eternal opposites or polarities. Just as in the Western system we have positive and negatives ascribed to the zodiac signs, within the Chinese system, we have yin and yang. Those interested in I Ching and Feng Shuei (covered by other books in this series), may already have an understanding of these symbols, which are usually drawn thus:

As you can see, yin and yang are a circle, divided into equal parts. Yang (white) represents day, summer, birth and light; yin (black) represents

black, winter, night and transition. You will also notice that there is a small point in each section, white in yin's blackness, and black in yang's whiteness, showing that opposite influences do indeed live in harmony.

These two opposites interact at all times, as do night and day, positive and negative, etc. The 12 animal emblems are broken down into two groups of six, one yin, the other yang. Ox, rabbit, snake, goat, rooster and pig are yin (passive). Rat, tiger, horse, dragon, monkey and dog are yang (active).

Some authorities will disagree with the above yin/yang categories and place the rat and dog in the yin category and the snake and rooster in the yang category. These authorities will also argue that the monkey and ox fall into both yin and yang categories equally. However, those given above are normally accepted as standard.

The yang person is usually very self-motivated and self-absorbed, serious in nature, calm yet fearing defeat. Quite a lively person, and good company, this person is likely to be very active and ambitious.

The yin person is usually introspective and introverted, preferring solitary pursuits to large gatherings of people. He is very discerning, yet compassionate and truthful. This person prefers his own company and to do his own thing. He is unlikely to take on a business partnership, preferring to work on projects alone, probably because he thinks his way is best. He usually generates a good reputation.

PRACTICE

So we have now taken our first steps in learning about Chinese horoscopes. We still have a lot to learn, but let's test ourselves on some of the points discussed. All answers will be found somewhere within the chapter, but are not given here. Best of luck!

- Tiger hours are 7pm-9pm. True or false?

- There are four elements associated with Chinese horoscopes. True or false?

- What planet is linked to the element of water?

- The sheep appears in every oriental system of astrology. True or false?

- The Chinese New Year always starts on 1 January of each year. True or false?

- The lion is one of the animals in the Chinese zodiac. True or false?

The Animal Signs

We are now going to start to look at each animal sign. We will not discuss in detail the elements associated with each year at this stage, although the elemental link will be given. This will be discussed later, when you have had a chance to absorb the basic information on the animal signs.

As we have already discovered, the Chinese New Year does not start on 1 January. Therefore, in the sections that follow, exact dates are given for each sign. Please read the appropriate section for your actual birth date.

This chapter gives information on each sign, together with details of famous people born under each sign, and lucky numbers. Please note, however, that lucky numbers don't necessarily mean lucky lottery numbers, etc., and you should still make your own decisions when using numbers in any form of gambling.

RAT

DATES

31 January	1900 –	18 February	1901	Metal Rat
18 February	1912 –	5 February	1913	Water Rat
5 February	1924 –	24 January	1925	Wood Rat
24 January	1936 –	10 February	1937	Fire Rat
10 February	1948 –	28 January	1949	Earth Rat
28 January	1960 –	14 February	1961	Metal Rat
15 February	1972 –	2 February	1973	Water Rat
2 February	1984 –	19 February	1985	Wood Rat
19 February	1996 –	6 February	1997	Fire Rat
6 February	2008 –	25 January	2009	Earth Rat

FAMOUS RATS

Prince Charles, Mata Hari, Richard Nixon, Shirley Bassey, William Shakespeare, Charlotte Brontë, Marlon Brando, Lauren Bacall, Tchaikovsky, Tolstoi, Strauss, Jimmy Carter, Vanessa Redgrave, Mozart, Dave Allen, Lawrence of Arabia, Andrew Lloyd Webber, Barbara Dickson, Prince Andrew.

LUCKY NUMBERS

1, 4, 5, 10, 11, 14, 41, 45, 51 and 54.

CHARACTER

If you are a rat, please don't feel this is a bad sign. Rats in the West are associated with plague, disease and pestilence, but to the Chinese, the rat is a nicer creature altogether.

Charming people, charismatic, intelligent and quick-witted, these people love to be in large groups, are fun-loving and sociable, and value friendships. To them friends are people whom they will always help, no matter what. With a wide circle of friends and acquaintances, they have long memories, and never forget. Rat people are well respected and well liked, but it takes time to get to know them properly. These people often waste opportunities, although they love to take risks. Gambling comes easy to them, but they are also fairly thrifty.

Looking good is important to the rat. If you are a rat you will have been naturally inquisitive from an early age. You are also naturally sexy and appealing. You like everything to move at a fast pace, and that includes conversation and travel – not forgetting cars. Anything slow and laborious is out. You especially like to steam through work, so that you have more time to play at the end of the day. Rats have messy handwriting because they are in such a hurry.

Criticism comes easily to the rat, and their opinions and instincts are normally right. They have the gift of intuition. They can normally sense things before they happen, and will often be found trying to help those of us who 'get taken for a ride', especially financially.

On first acquaintance, despite their obvious appeal, people often think the rat is a brash, swaggering character, but this is not the case, as they are very compassionate, yet feel the need to hide this behind a tough exterior. They do this so that they can decide whether or not their new friend can be trusted.

Rats make good detectives and spies – Mata Hari was a rat. They also seem intrigued by the arcane sciences. They seem to follow their instinct and love to hear the latest news, especially if it involves somebody's success. These people strike while the iron is hot. Never underestimate the rat, as they are very tenacious. They like to lead, and can be very pushy at times. Takeover bids are very easy for the rat. They bide their time, then strike when it is least expected.

Rats are party people, hardly ever sit still, and love discos. They seem to come alive after dark. Rats love to talk, and can be quite verbose. Their need to talk things through is a fundamental part of their character. Even if depressed, rat people need to talk their problem through with someone. They need feedback, and sometimes an audience, but other people can have a problem getting a word in edgeways. All the stresses to which they are subject can be released at night, and you can often find the lovelorn rat relating chapter and verse to close friends well into the early hours. Rat people have no sense of time and often break appointments because they are involved somewhere else. All this activity can take its toll, and rats need to learn how to recharge their batteries. They should also watch what they eat at parties and late at night, as dietary and weight problems can result.

ReLATIONShIPS

Those people who live with the rat will know that they are often very secretive people, sometimes finding it necessary to bottle things up inside, especially if the hurt goes deep. They will even lie rather than reveal their desires and wishes. Emotionally, rats find it difficult to give. As with possessions, rats are hoarders of anything personal to them. These people are very romantic, sensual and deep, and they will defend their loved ones, no matter what. Seduction techniques might have been invented by the rat, to whom the sexual side of love is very important.

Their need to be King or Queen in their home environment means the rat person will often pick a partner who can be dominated, or who they perceive to be weaker than themselves. That brings many problems, not least of which is the fact that they often find themselves despising their partner, and abandoning them for someone more appealing. Unfortunately rat people sometimes use others for their own ends, although they rarely set out to hurt other people deliberately. They do, however, hate people who nag or who seem to be content to live in less than tidy and clean environments. They won't spend a fortune on their home – they might move. Those living with a rat must be prepared to have late nights. The rat person seems to come awake at midnight with new ideas, which of course need talking through before bedtime.

Their occasional inability to see the other person's viewpoint or take their needs into account can cause problems. They are very impatient, with active minds and imaginations. Rat people (as with the rats in the Pied Piper story) are often led astray by people whose motives are suspect, possibly because of their overwhelming sense of loyalty. However, the rat person will bounce back.

Female rats are good at organising parties, but equally good with their children. They need their own career, and like to give their youngsters free rein, but they don't go short of affection or understanding.

CAREER AND MONEY

Rats need to be involved in a lot of things at the same time, including efforts to help others within their community. They don't like to think that they are missing out on anything! One of the problems with this is that they often get involved in too many things at once and consequently find themselves with insufficient energy for the project in hand. Rats should try to concentrate on one project at a time and see it through to the end before starting on something else.

Good partners in business, these people can often save failing businesses, and thrive on anything to do with advertising or promotion. They are also very good with figures, so make excellent accountants and financial planners, as well as lawyers and executives. Communication is one of their fortes, and they love novelty, so they may do well in journalism or some other form of writing. Politics is another career area for them to consider.

Not terribly practical, rats are ideas people. They can solve problems, but they may be unable to finish the task in hand.

Money can cause a problem for the rat, who can both save and spend at the same time. One minute they seem to save hard, and the next minute they spend like millionaires. The need to have something put aside for a rainy day never leaves the rat person, although spending sprees hold a great fascination. However, don't expect the rat person to keep records of spending, as they won't. Generous friends, these people will lend you anything – except money.

Both male and female rats love shopping, are great at spotting a bargain, and appreciate and expect good food and comfortable surroundings. Rat people have great aspirations, and their entrepreneurial streak often leads them to great riches. Failing that, they will naturally gravitate towards people who have the things they themselves desire, and then will happily 'name -drop' to anybody within shouting distance.

health and well-being

Often anxiety will get the better of the rat person, and they will spend time alone thinking things through. They are nervous, fidgety types who play with rubber bands and paperclips under the table so that their companions have no idea of their nerves. They often succumb to stress-related illness and hypochondria. Often fearing themselves to be failures, they are very hard on themselves. They should watch their tempers when times get tough, as sudden outbursts of anger can be quite frightening to those close to them. They will shout and rage with their partners, yet they get easily upset themselves.

dates

19 February 1901	–	7 February 1902	Metal Ox
6 February 1913	–	25 January 1914	Water Ox
24 January 1925	–	12 February 1926	Wood Ox
11 February 1937	–	30 January 1938	Fire Ox
29 January 1949	–	16 February 1950	Earth Ox
15 February 1961	–	4 February 1962	Metal Ox
3 February 1973	–	22 January 1974	Water Ox
20 February 1985	–	8 February 1986	Wood Ox
7 February 1997	–	27 January 1998	Fire Ox
26 January 2009	–	13 February 2010	Earth Ox

FAMOUS OXEN

Frank Bruno, Napoleon Bonaparte, Barbara Cartland, Peter Sellers, Paul Newman, Emperor Hirohito, J. S. Bach, Twiggy, George Gershwin, Robert Redford, The Princess of Wales, Hans Christian Andersen, Jane Fonda, Walt Disney, Meryl Streep, Adolf Hitler, Margaret Thatcher.

LUCKY NUMBERS

1, 3, 5, 12, 15, 33, 35, 51 and 53.

CHARACTER

Stable, sensible, solid, determined, strong and tenacious, these people have integrity and strength of purpose and are reliable and true to the end. Reserved, contemplative and unpretentious, they make excellent friends and partners, and they will always be there for their friends in a crisis, offering sensible and logical advice. These are the people beavering away in the background, rather than seeking the limelight.

Probably because of their calm approach, they tend to live to a ripe old age. You can be sure they will see things through to the end, unlike the rat, although they may moan about it. They can be really grumpy on occasion. As a result, a rat–ox partnership will be successful, once both have realised their need for each other. Oxen make good managers, because of their need for routine and method, as well as their materialism, whilst the rat will be the ideas person. However, don't expect any flexibility here, as the ox will not be able to deal with that.

RELATIONSHIPS

Outsiders will often view the ox person as lacking in humour, yet will be attracted to their reliability. Doing things 'for the hell of it' just isn't the ox's scene. Oxen are slow to anger, and will let problems and upsets simmer for a long time before they finally explode.

They make excellent – if somewhat bossy – parents, and children and the home are always very important to them. Even when the ox has married and moved away, their own parents will still be important, and it is not unheard of for the ox to have his or her elderly parent(s) move in with the rest of the family. Oxen are often brilliant cooks, who also love making their own clothes.

Physical and attractive, these people are very earthy in relationships, although they can be lacking in imagination, and male oxen need to be prodded into buying flowers or chocolates for their special person. However, a need for self-protection means that nobody really knows what's going on inside the ox. They find it difficult to get over broken relationships.

CAREER AND MONEY

Ox people take their duties very seriously indeed, and they will frown on any sign of frivolity in a work environment. The ox doesn't like novelties and gimmicks, and they can be very critical of such things. Give an ox something to do, and he or she will happily work on it totally unaided until it has been completed to their satisfaction.

These are truly organised people, although some would say they are pigeon-holed. People who don't pull their weight at work will irritate the ox, as will those whose time-keeping is not up to standard. Punctuality is important to the ox: employees of ox bosses take note.

Stubborn and steadfast, ox people will rarely take risks, preferring the sure route, the tried and tested methods, rather than anything new or adventurous. Ox people don't feel comfortable with change. They often stick with things for a long time because of this need for stability. In business situations, this can often cause problems, as the ox person will not understand the need to try new ideas. Ox people take time to make decisions, weighing up all the pros and cons before taking even the first step, and hate competitive situations.

Their need for security is paramount to their very existence, and they always have money put aside for emergencies. However, they

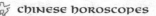 

can become greedy and money can become a big issue in their lives.

Quite happy to carry out their own renovation work at home, the ox person may also be quite capable of building their home themselves, often choosing somewhere rural, as they hate large conurbations. These are practical people who are very clever with their hands, and take their time making sure everything is properly done. They will also be good gardeners, and a tidy and neat garden is a sure sign of the ox at work. Never rush an ox, as it important for them to take their time.

The warmth of the ox person towards his fellow man or woman is an endearing trait, and although they often seem boring to other signs because of their need for stability, they are genuine and sincere. They care about other people, and can often be found in organisations that work for humanity or the environment. They also make excellent politicians, geologists and farmers. They enjoy outdoor pursuits and holidays, such as camping and hiking. Other jobs where the ox will thrive include planning, finance and development or anything requiring skills, such as carpentry or craft work. They may not say much, but when they do, they are eloquent speakers. Many writers are oxen.

These are serious, undemonstrative, even-tempered and patient people, often totally lacking in tenderness, who will stick with something even if they are, deep down, aware that they have made a big mistake. U-turns are not for them. These people are also terrible losers. They become sullen if things don't go according to their plan, and they often blame others for their own mistakes, and they never forgive.

Oxen can be terrible bigots, petty, vindictive, biased and authoritarian. Male oxen can also be very chauvinistic. One of the best ways to upset an ox is to tell them that you consider them solid, cautious and dependable, which of course is exactly what they are. They prefer to be thought of as exciting, daring and original. They are earthy and unromantic, but can't see this in themselves.

health and well-being

Oxen can often be terribly uncompromising. They need to learn

flexibility. They are also very possessive, and this can cause problems. They are difficult people to get to know, and to live with, and few can say they know the ox well, because they have a tendency towards introversion. They prefer peace, tranquillity and quiet to the high life, and as such are not party people and can be seen as unsociable. Travel may also not appeal, probably because of their dislike of change in climate, as they feel the cold terribly. They also react badly in very hot climates. Oxen have huge appetites, and they need to pay attention to their diet. Sweet things may prove a big temptation.

TIGER

Dates

8 February 1902 – 28 January 1903			Water Tiger
26 January 1914 – 13 February 1915			Wood Tiger
13 February 1926 – 1 February 1927			Fire Tiger
31 January 1938 – 18 February 1939			Earth Tiger
17 February 1950 – 5 February 1951			Metal Tiger
23 January 1974 – 10 February 1975			Wood Tiger
5 February 1962 – 24 January 1963			Water Tiger
9 February 1986 – 28 January 1987			Fire Tiger
28 January 1998 – 15 February 1999			Earth Tiger
14 February 2010 – 2 February 2011			Metal Tiger

FAMOUS TIGERS

Oscar Wilde, Princess Anne, Agatha Christie, Terry Wogan, Paul Daniels, Beethoven, Richard Branson, Marilyn Monroe, Marie Curie, Dylan Thomas, Karl Marx, Charles de Gaulle, Ho Chi Minh, Charles Lindbergh.

LUCKY NUMBERS

4, 5, 7, 9, 13, 34, 44, 45 and 54.

CHARACTER

Forceful, compulsive, brave, lucky, magnetic, unrestrained, intense, moody, aggressive and ferocious, these people are direct, outspoken and straightforward. Although they are warm-hearted and generous, making an enemy of a Tiger is not to be recommended. They have a very loud roar, and seem to blow up without warning. They won't be pushed around under any circumstances. They can be very rebellious. They hate pretension and injustice.

Sometimes tigers will come across as big-headed, know-it-all types, whose ego is only matched by their showy sense of dress and behaviour. They aren't bothered about fashion, but they certainly know how to make themselves noticed. Underneath all that, however, is someone who misses nothing, smiles and learns from what is going on around them, and who uses situations to their own ends.

There is something compelling about the Tiger person, yet their single-mindedness, competitive nature and ambition can grate with those of us who are less dynamic.

Tigers hate to be restrained. They must be free to wander and investigate. Any rules must be theirs, and not other people's. Proud and brave, they fear nothing and nobody, and will happily enter into situations that others would avoid. Risk-taking is something the tiger loves, as they are naturally impetuous. They can also be terribly hot-headed. Conventional things will hold little or no interest. This

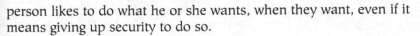

person likes to do what he or she wants, when they want, even if it means giving up security to do so.

Sometimes this impulsive streak can lead the tiger to regret his or her actions. Jumping in with both feet often causes the tiger problems in later life. Bouts of melancholy will result at such times, and there is nothing worse than an unhappy tiger. However, as maturity develops, the tiger person comes to realise that life isn't all a bed of roses, and can become quite philosophical about the whole issue.

Once a tiger has made a decision, they will hold fast to it, as if giving it up would be something dreadful. They will stick with their beliefs no matter what, even arguing that black is white if that is what they think at the time.

Female tigers are also brilliant hostesses. Neat, tidy, looking totally unflustered and calm, this is the woman who seems to have everything under control, the children bathed and in bed, and all choices of food and wine offered.

Relationships

The family will always be a refuge for the tiger, somewhere comfortable, tasteful and uncluttered. It is to their homes that they retreat at the end of a stressful day. There they still rule the roost. That doesn't mean, however, that they won't want to hear the latest gossip, as this is something most tigers love, whether male or female.

Quick-witted and charming, they make excellent hosts, and an evening spent with a tiger can be quite an experience! Both male and female tigers are great with children, theirs or anybody's for that matter! Great storytellers, popular babysitters and often exceptional teachers, these people won't bother too much if their children don't do all their homework, as long as they can show that they are learning something.

Jealousy is something which besets most tigers. They are fiercely protective of their family, their friends and their home. They can also

be extremely intense and possessive, and stifle those with whom they live. Yet while they expect their partner to be faithful, they are often less so themselves.

Take them to a party and introduce them to the latest model from a glossy magazine, and you stand a chance of losing them for ever. They are restless people to whom an evening in can seem like a prison sentence. They dislike their own company and will take any chance to be out with other people.

Most tigers love parties. They like having fun, love good food and good company, and also like to be the centre of attention. They are entertaining, humorous and witty companions, and most of all great fun to be with. If you're feeling down, make a date with a tiger. You'll certainly come back happier, even if totally exhausted.

CAREER ANO (MONEY

Give a tiger a job to do and they will set about it with great energy. They seem to thrive on challenge and are very hardworking. New ideas, new incentives and new courses of action are always of interest to the tiger, and their enthusiasm knows no bounds. Tigers love variety and change, and will often hold down several jobs, all of them different, in order to provide that necessary variety.

Tigers succeed in most endeavours, especially those which require energy, such as journalism, dance and the armed forces. Tigers of both sexes certainly know how to fight. Other career areas to which they are suited include medicine and science. Female tigers, whilst being excellent mothers, may also need their own career to give them sufficient financial independence from their mate.

Likely to move about a lot, these people are nevertheless quite indecisive at times. Advice offered at such times will be ignored, as the tiger doesn't like to ask for support. He feels it threatens his independence. He can be very obstinate at such times.

These people are born to lead and are full of ideas. They take orders badly and are very restless. Things which demand detail and moving around paper on a desk are not for them. The tiger expects to be paid well for his work, and knows how to spend money too.

Generous to a fault, this person will shower his partner with expensive gifts should the mood take him, and never think of putting something into a savings account. Money is to be enjoyed – that's the tiger philosophy.

Tigers are sometimes seen as rebels, and are often unpopular. Despite this, they often rise to high rank because of their boundless energy and enthusiasm, and their ability to deal with a multitude of things at the same time. Both sexes follow the same pattern – they need to look good, have their independence, and be admired.

health and well-being

Most tigers are keen sportspeople or at the very least like some form of exercise. They need to look good and appreciate the need to keep fit as part of their overall appearance. Tigers care what people think of them and the initial impression matters a great deal. As a result, they invariably have good posture, and will know all about positioning themselves in a room to the best advantage. They are there to be seen and they will make sure that they are. Tigers are good at getting attention, whether for themselves or for causes they support.

Tigers love their food, and need to watch what they eat, and the speed at which they eat it. Eating on the run seems to come naturally to the tiger, and they should learn to relax more, especially after a large meal.

PRACTICE

We have now covered the first three animal signs. It is again time to test our knowledge. As usual the answers will not be given, but will be found somewhere in the chapter.

- The tiger person is unassuming and quiet. True or false?

- Rat people like early nights. True or false?

- Ox people are very sensual and romantic, and shower their partners with expensive presents. True or false?

- Female oxen love impromptu shopping sprees. True or false?

- Most comedians and revolutionaries are oxen. Is this likely?

- Rat people will hoard things. True or false?

- Beethoven was a Tiger. True or false?

We have covered the first three animal signs, and we are now moving on to look at a further three, namely the rabbit, the dragon and the snake. Again, the basic character traits are given for each sign. The elemental variations are listed here, and described in Chapter 3.

RABBIT

Dates

29 January	1903 –	15 February	1904	Water Rabbit
14 February	1915 –	2 February	1916	Wood Rabbit
2 February	1927 –	22 January	1928	Fire Rabbit
19 February	1939 –	7 February	1940	Earth Rabbit
6 February	1951 –	26 January	1952	Metal Rabbit
25 January	1963 –	12 February	1964	Water Rabbit
11 February	1975 –	30 January	1976	Wood Rabbit
29 January	1987 –	16 February	1988	Fire Rabbit
16 February	1999 –	4 February	2000	Earth Rabbit
3 February	2011 –	22 January	2012	Metal Rabbit

Famous Rabbits

Prince Albert, Patrick Lord Lichfield, Eva Peron, Queen Victoria, Rudolph Nureyev, David Frost, Ken Dodd, Confucius, Andy Warhol, Orson Welles.

Lucky Numbers

1, 3, 5, 9, 15, 19 and 35

Character

The rabbit person is sociable, kind, compassionate and humble, and most probably artistic or at least creative in some way, though rarely ostentatious. Chic, refined, tactful yet ambitious, they are complex people, sometimes secretive and pedantic, and prone to bouts of hypochondria. Rabbits are sensitive souls, rather mercurial, with the gift of foresight and intuition, and are said to be born to live rich and fortunate lives. Traditionally this is also the fertility symbol of the animal signs, and it is said that the rabbit is also the symbol of immortality.

Discos are not rabbits' favourite places. They are more at home discussing history or art, listening to classical music or enjoying a fine meal. These people like comfort and elegance, and appreciate the theatre, although they dislike opening nights and prefer to go to the show when everyone else has already been.

Totally non-belligerent, they seem to accept their fate, no matter what. They are, however, very astute and cunning, and will seize opportunities, although not always with resulting success. They always seem to be in the right place at the right time. Don't expect the rabbit person, however, to take quick decisions, especially if the situation is tense. This is something most rabbits hate. Nor do they adjust easily to change.

They like traditional things and customary behaviour. Anything new, including new people, can make the rabbit nervous. Rabbits whether men or women, are likely to be caring, nurturing types, family people who are thoughtful, sympathetic and considerate. This is the person you can always turn to for understanding, and others will be drawn to them for this reason. Rabbit people are very discreet, and won't tell anybody something told to them in confidence.

The rabbit home is likely to be important to them, comfortable and well ordered, and with all the latest gadgets, computers, hi-fi equipment, etc. They will also have quite a good library: the rabbit likes to read. Lady rabbits are good hostesses, and seem to be able to manage to whip up a feast with very little prior warning, and still find time to sit and chat to the guests.

Rabbits expect and adore good food, and a trip to a restaurant with a rabbit is likely to prove an expensive night out. This is also another sign which loves to shop, especially for personal or cosmetic items and expensive clothes. Although they are somewhat self-indulgent, they are resilient people. They will keep working towards their goal irrespective of hurdles, despite the fact that they hate complications and much prefer the even pathway. Rabbits enjoy outdoor activities, They take the time to learn about their environment, are sensitive to it and never leave litter or mess. They may dislike travel, but if planning to go abroad they will read up about their destination beforehand, and then want to see all the museums, art galleries and cultural centres once they get there.

ReLATIONSHIPS

Rabbits are not tactile people – they will visibly shy away from hugs

and outward shows of affection. They may seem rather aloof, but they are really very friendly people. They listen politely when in conversation, and can be relied on to remember all the details. They like to gossip.

Close emotional ties can often prove problematical for the rabbit, who likes to be a part of a group but apart from it. However, they love to be pampered.

Rabbits hate violence and brutality. In fact, they dislike confrontation and unpleasantness of any kind. They will go to great lengths to avoid an argument and are likely to be pacifist by nature. They will probably not want to get involved in anything which doesn't affect them personally. They have a great knack of getting out of trouble, and whilst they often recognise problems and sympathise with causes, they may not actually help directly.

Despite their desire to remain in the background, rabbit people love a good discussion, although they often keep criticism to themselves as they don't want to rock the boat. They often get hurt, and will, at those times, strike out verbally, using sarcasm to disguise their wounded feelings.

Rabbits make good parents, bestowing love and discipline in equal store. Their children are well dressed and well behaved: rabbit parents stand for no nonsense.

CAREER AND MONEY

Don't ask a rabbit for a loan, because rabbit people are very careful with their money and reluctant to part with it, unless they can be sure you will return it on the due date, possibly with interest. They will always repay a debt on time, and expect everyone else to be like them. If the rabbit person feels they owe you a debt of gratitude, they will most certainly repay you.

Tactful and diplomatic, they will offer their counsel when the time is right, and not before. They often seem wise beyond their years, and can draw people together in a common bond, often because of their brilliant sense of humour. Not great joke-tellers, they are nevertheless witty people, and as such, they are great conciliators.

They make good diplomats, doctors, nurses, teachers, personnel officers, administrators, counsellors, priests and lawyers. Many rabbit people find themselves working with children or animals, or both, especially if a charitable cause is involved. Although loyal employees, they have set timetables for work, and shouldn't be expected to work too long or to expend too much physical effort. They sometimes put their social life before work.

health and well-being

Rabbits suffer from stress-related stomach problems. They can also be made ill by loud noises, flashing lights, smoke and dirt.

DRAGON

dates

16 February	1904 –	3 February	1905	Wood Dragon
4 February	1916 –	22 January	1917	Fire Dragon
23 January	1928 –	9 February	1929	Earth Dragon
8 February	1940 –	26 January	1941	Metal Dragon
27 January	1952 –	13 February	1953	Water Dragon
13 February	1964 –	1 February	1965	Wood Dragon
31 January	1976 –	17 February	1977	Fire Dragon
17 February	1988 –	5 February	1989	Earth Dragon
5 February	2000 –	23 January	2001	Metal Dragon
23 January	2012 –	9 February	2013	Water Dragon

FAMOUS DRAGONS

Harold Wilson, Joan of Arc, George Bernard Shaw, Martin Luther King, Lewis Carroll, Cary Grant, Florence Nightingale, Jimmy Connors, Cliff Richard, Ringo Starr, Che Guevara, Prince Edward.

LUCKY NUMBERS

3, 4, 5, 6, 15, 21, 34, 35, 36 and 45.

CHARACTER

These people are adaptable, yet quite volatile, especially when given orders, as they dislike being told what to do (as a dragon, I can vouch for that!). They are self-sufficient and cherish their independence. It is said that you can always spot a dragon, because they never shut up. However, they are also quite magnetic personalities, and command attention, even if you dislike them.

These people are showmen. They have a dignity which can sometimes be mistaken for pomposity. As a result, they have few really close friends, but lots of acquaintances. They are vital, lively, restless, intelligent, strong-willed and decisive, and sometimes they can be over-confident and appear brash and pushy.

Quick-tempered and blunt, they often hurt others with their attitude, especially dragon ladies, who can be very domineering and forthright. This lady really does want it all, and want it now. Patience isn't a strong point with her. They often think they know it all, and often they do – though sometimes they are totally wrong.

Honesty is all that matters to the dragon, and sometimes they don't think about what they are saying and how it will be taken by others before opening their mouths. If they think they have hurt someone, they are full of remorse at their tactlessness. if you have been hurt by a dragon, just cry. Dragons hate to see tears, and are really very sentimental. However, don't overdo it, because they can spot a fake. If a dragon promises something, they mean it, and they expect others to be likewise. Consequently they are sometimes too trusting.

Underneath it all, dragons merely need to be wanted, and need praise for their efforts, as they are very insecure and nervous, even though outwardly they appear so confident and capable. Many dragons find their way into entertainment (especially comedy, as they are naturally witty and whimsical), where they can see at once when their work is appreciated. Dragons have a way of attracting publicity and attention. Female dragons will be very idealistic, but will always put their family and close friends before themselves and their ambitions, even looking on it as a duty.

Once they have made up their mind on something (or someone) they will stick to their chosen path, even if it seems totally stupid to do so.

Dragons are hardworking people, who take on lots of tasks and seem to have boundless energy. They expect perfection, which can result in their being hypercritical, although they themselves cannot take criticism at all. They can be blunt to the point of rudeness, but they are really only trying to be honest.

Great to have on your side, especially in difficult situations, and wonderful champions of causes, dragons are not to be tackled lightly once in full flight. The environment and its protection will be important to the dragon person.

These are no-nonsense people, irrespective of gender, and they don't like to admit to being wrong. Dragon people do not suffer fools gladly, and it shows in their faces when they dislike someone. Dragons dislike delay and are good timekeepers, expecting others to be the same. They are also rather impulsive and often rush into things without the required forethought. Two dragons together don't make good partners.

Their energy level, which is quite high, will often run in fits and starts. These are fast/stop people, with nothing in between, and they have problems working to a schedule. As a result they sometimes leave things unfinished.

Good listeners, they will help whenever asked, and will rarely talk much in new company. Once they feel comfortable, they will talk a lot, normally about themselves or matters close to their heart.

Dragons have a habit of getting themselves noticed, though not always at the right time. It might be worth noting, at this point, that the dragon is the only mythical creature in the Chinese system, all other animals being ordinary creatures, Maybe this says something about the dragon – they are certainly original. The downside of this is that they sometimes come across as completely eccentric and odd, with egotistical traits and a dogmatic personality.

Chinese tradition states that the dragon is a lucky creature, and it follows that dragon people are often lucky. They are also often blessed with long lives, whilst maintaining a youthful attitude and approach to life. As they get older, they tend to gravitate more to younger groups of people, with whom they often feel they have more in common.

Anything esoteric or philosophical is likely to appeal to the dragon, who is naturally intuitive and sensitive, although they are quite discriminatory and perceptive. Ask a dragon to help solve a problem, and you can expect an unorthodox solution, but one which will work, given a chance. Likewise, their intuitive streak may often see them abandon logic and do something apparently out of character, until you fully understand the dragon's mind.

The home will always be important to the dragon, although often only as a base from which to travel, and they are very protective of their families. They like to spend money especially on their homes.

Relationships

Sometimes dragons get infatuated with other people, put them on a pedestal and refuse to see the reality of the situation, especially in romantic matters. When they do fall in love, however, they fall hard, as they are very sentimental types. Their love will be their life, and partners and loved ones can get away with murder on occasion, They can seldom see faults in those they care about.

Popular with the opposite sex, despite their plain and simple dress and appearance, jealousy is an alien feeling for dragons, and they rarely feel jealous about anything or anybody. Female dragons are said to be particularly highly sexed and to need a lot of attention.

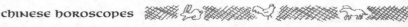

CAREER AND money

Dragons are well-organised, logical people (some would say they think too much), and have high standards, both for themselves and for others. They are also ambitious, and they make excellent leaders (they do lead the Chinese New Year procession). They can often be found working in politics, teaching, counselling, sales or advertising/promotion. Other careers for the dragon would include working with the soil, as an archaeologist, geologist, gem expert, housing developer or even a jeweller.

Dragons are often lucky with money.

health AND well-being

Stress can prove to be a major problem for the dragon, who suffers bouts of depression and stomach problems as a result of their inward anxieties and insecurities. These people are big eaters, and also suffer with respiratory problems, sinus attacks, asthma, etc.

These people need lots of love and affection. Their natural reserve can be mistaken for coldness, but they are intense and romantic people who need lots of cuddles and hugs to function well on a daily basis. They also need to be told that other people care, even if deep down they really know all the time.

SNAKE

蛇

dates

4 February	1905 – 24 January	1906	Wood Snake
23 January	1917 – 10 February	1918	Fire Snake
10 February	1929 – 29 January	1930	Earth Snake
27 January	1941 – 14 February	1942	Metal Snake
14 February	1953 – 2 February	1954	Water Snake
2 February	1965 – 20 January	1966	Wood Snake
18 February	1977 – 6 February	1978	Fire Snake
6 February	1989 – 26 January	1990	Earth Snake
24 January	2001 – 11 February	2002	Metal Snake
10 February	2013 – 30 January	2014	Water Snake

famous snakes

Mahatma Ghandi, Charles Darwin, Abraham Lincoln, Bob Dylan, Michael Crawford, John Paul Getty, J. F. Kennedy, Mao Tse-tung, Aristotle and Jacqueline Onassis.

lucky numbers

1, 2, 4, 6, 13, 24, 42 and 46.

character

These people seem to know a lot about many subjects, but are really very reserved, naive and easily shocked. Well read, and with a retentive memory for many subjects, snake people will have an ingrained love of books, museums and cultural buildings. Wise and discreet, they make good friends, but can be very presumptive on occasion, and demand exclusivity from their friends. They are elegant, direct yet subtle, gregarious, dissembling and prudent.

The Chinese consider snakes to be guardians of buried treasure, and as such they have always been considered good omens and symbols of wisdom and cleverness.

They often make the best of situations by their active, adaptable and forceful nature, although they are often likely to be selfish and a

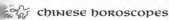 
little lazy, especially the female snake. They are prepared to wait for opportunities rather than try to create them.

They are the master/mistress of understatement. They like gossip, although they hate small talk, are very moralistic, and are never idle, often feeling responsible for their friends, family and associates. These are intuitive, philosophical thinkers and shrewd financiers.

Relationships

Snakes are jealous, possessive and loyal, especially where family are concerned. Nobody is quite so possessive with friends and family as the snake. They choose their friends with caution, and treat them generously. They flatter their friends and expect equal amounts of flattery in return. They can sulk for hours if they feel they are being ignored or have failed in any endeavour. They are bad losers.

It is wise to respect a snake, as you never really know where you stand with them. Because of this fact, many people fear them, as they seem to shed their emotions like their animal counterpart sheds its skin. They play their cards very close to their chests, and are private people, appearing to be quiet and passive. They seem to conspire and argue, yet they are precise and secretive. Don't expect a snake to share their innermost feelings with you, because they won't, even if you are part of the family. They often seem to get their way by making others think that the idea was theirs in the first place. They are the plotters amongst us. To cross a snake is a mistake: their bite is lethal. They are also astute at detecting falsehood, and they don't take kindly to anyone who lies to them.

The snake person is a lively companion, with a ready and penetrating wit, although they may dislike large social gatherings. Ostentation is not for them. They like quiet and calm, but are very passionate underneath and quite sexy. Snakes of both sexes love to be in love. They are sentimental, and even smothering. They may have extramarital affairs, too, but expect their partner to be faithful.

Career and Money

Shopping in the sales is definitely not the snake's scene. They much

prefer exclusive shops; for them, spending money holds no fears, and they believe that 'you get what you pay for'. These people like accessories, but they have to be the best they can buy. Elegant surroundings appeal to them, as they appreciate the finer things in life. They like to be seen in the best places, preferably before the rest of the world gets there. They expect the best of all things and to be treated as extra-special. They happily spend money on expensive presents, yet they may be less affluent than they seem.

Snakes are not innovators. They are conservative people who like to see how things go before making a commitment. Making decisions does not come easy to them at all, although they will be the first to express their likes and dislikes.

Snakes are hard workers once they manage to get going in the morning, and very reliable. Once they start a project, they will see it through to the end. These people never miss much, and always seem to know what is going on, where to lay their hands on things and what little extra touches will bring about the best result.

Good with money, they rarely let other people know their financial state, and are also very secretive when it comes to emotional issues. They are therefore good at wheeling and dealing, although they make terrible gamblers.

Snake careers include doctor, dentist, detective, researcher, teacher, artist, designer, accountancy, scientist, writer and engineer. However, they hate being too much in the public eye.

ʜᴇᴀʟᴛʜ ᴀɴᴅ ᴡᴇʟʟ-ʙᴇɪɴɢ

Snake people tend to suffer with their nerves, which are extremely fragile, and they don't enjoy the best of health. They are always on the go (at their own pace) and when they stop, they are invariably exhausted. They don't know how to relax, and even when they realise they need time away from work, they will fill spare hours with trips out to various places. Even on holiday they are planning what to do next. Because they are unable to relax, blood pressure problems are often apparent.

They also need a calm environment in which to live and work – not for them the bustle of the stock exchange or anywhere where there is noise, dirt or indeed anything stressful. Snakes like to be at home more than out socialising.

PRACTICE

We have now covered a further three animal signs. Before we go on we should see how much we have assimilated. Again, the answers are all in the text.

- Dragon people are very reserved and quiet. True or false?

- Two dragons together make a good partnership. True or false?

- Which animal leads the procession at Chinese New Year celebrations?

- The rabbit person will always lead the way, rather than work in the background. True or false?

- The snake person is likely to be found in the entertainment world. True or false?

- Andy Warhol was a dragon. True or false?

- Snakes are considered by the Chinese to be unlucky and evil creatures. True or false?

On we go with the next three animal signs, which are the horse, goat and monkey. Remember that some texts may refer to the sheep rather than the goat. We are sticking to the original animal emblems here, but the characteristics are the same.

HORSE

DATES

25 January	1906 –	12 February 1907	Fire Horse
11 February	1918 –	31 January 919	Earth Horse
30 January	1930 –	16 February 1931	Metal Horse
15 February	1942 –	4 February 1943	Water Horse
3 February	1954 -	23 January 1955	Wood Horse
21 January	1966 –	8 February 1967	Fire Horse
7 February	1978 –	27 January 1979	Earth Horse
27 January	1990 –	14 February 1991	Metal Horse
12 February	2002 –	31 January 2003	Water Horse
31 January	2014 –	18 February 2015	Wood Horse

FAMOUS HORSES

Muhammed Ali, Lenin, Frederick Chopin, Clint Eastwood, Lord Snowdon, Barbra Streisand, Jimi Hendrix, Genghis Khan, Isaac Newton, Buffalo Bill Cody.

LUCKY NUMBERS

1, 3, 4, 8, 13, 14, 41 and 43.

CHARACTER

These sporty people, who love travel and movement, are sociable, good-looking, healthy, extrovert, energetic and smart. Strong-willed

and skilful, they can be terribly prejudiced, blunt and intolerant, and not above placing themselves first, most of the time. The key word for these people is, however, style: they have lots of it.

Good conversationalists, these people aren't above a bit of gossip. They also enjoy a good debate, but don't tell them a secret if you want it to stay one. Young horses can be particularly difficult to tame, as they feel obliged to express themselves in their own way at every opportunity. Most horses are, irrespective of age, easily distracted and lacking in focus at times, and become easily bored.

Horses often feel they are right on every issue, and will fight tooth and nail before giving up their freedom. In China, female horses are said to become bossy wives.

Horses seem to have a natural flair for leadership, and usually have a wide circle of friends. They like to be the centre of attention, and they hate being ignored. They also hate people who fawn or who talk rubbish. On such occasions, the horse's tongue is lethal.

They are enthusiastic people, restless, pragmatic , independent, impatient and easily frustrated, but very active and quick to take up any new challenge. Horse people seldom plan for their old age – anything long-term holds little interest. As we will see later, those born as fire horses are said to be revolutionaries and tyrants, and most horses have a fair bit of aggression and like to take risks. Horses make good soldiers, but bad diplomats, as they are far too outspoken. The horse person is dependable, helpful and trustworthy, and expects the same of his friends.

Horses seem to know what is going to be said before the other person opens their mouth. They will often sum up what you intended to say a whole lot better than you would have done.

Lady horses are very well turned out. Nothing shoddy or jaded for them – only the best will do, and boy do they know how to steal a scene! Male horses are a little less ostentatious, but again they know how to dress. Quite vain underneath it all, these elegant people have a very original sense of humour, can speak to large groups and gatherings without fear, and work methodically yet speedily on all tasks.

Making snap decisions is very much the horse's forte. What's more, their decision is invariably the right one, and they won't be heard moaning about other people making too many demands of them.

Horse people are good at putting together a brilliant party, with a wide variety of different people, different foods and drinks (lots of food, often quite exotic), and a good cross-section of music. They get bored with things being the same all the time, and go out of their way to create variety.

ReLATIONShIps

Interference in their personal lives is something the horse will not tolerate. At such times they can be very sharp. They look after their families, their way. Love is sometimes a difficult path for the horse, because they are very strong-willed and can often be intolerant of their partner's feelings. However, given time they can learn to compromise.

They take broken romances badly, and will never admit to having any failings. They are faithful people, yet can be very hot-headed, prone to sarcastic outbursts, condescending remarks and sullen moods when upset. At such times, they will seem to shut themselves off to everyone and everything.

They also suffer from bouts of anxiety and can be very unscrupulous when they want their own way. Horse people fall in love easily, yet often find relationships problematical, probably because of their tendency towards idealism in this area, and the need to follow their own interests when it suits. Horses often have several marriages before finding the right partner. They seem to gravitate towards partners who are already involved with other people – to their eventual regret.

Whatever you do, never make a horse look ridiculous in public. Humiliation is something the horse cannot stand. You will remember the resulting outburst to your dying day, even if the horse later apologises. At other times, you may expect an outburst, only to find that the horse merely walks away without saying anything.

CAREER AND MONEY

Horses are ambitious and competitive. Their ideal career areas include leisure and sport (they excel in most sports), travel and entertainment, invention, exploration, design, management, public relations and acting. As they are good with their hands, they also make excellent builders, craftworkers and engineers. They are also keen on travel, and may therefore be interested in foreign trade. However, they may find climatic changes a problem.

Good, responsible employees, with a ready wit, these people often earn substantial sums of money. They will work long and hard, sometimes well into the night, to get a job finished, but sometimes find themselves rushing. Horses are very organised and seem to have unlimited energy. They never give up on a project, even if ill.

These people seem to take everything in their stride. To them a hurdle is just something to be cleared before passing the winning post.

HEALTH AND WELL-BEING

Health problems can often result from the horse's tendency to overindulge, and they also suffer from stress-related problems. However, for the most part, they are healthy people.

GOAT

Dates

13 February 1907 – 1 February 1908	Fire Goat
1 February 1919 – 19 February 1920	Earth Goat
17 February 1931 – 5 February 1932	Metal Goat
5 February 1943 – 24 January 1944	Water Goat
24 January 1955 – 11 February 1956	Wood Goat
9 February 1967 – 29 January 1968	Fire Goat
28 January 1979 – 15 February 1980	Earth Goat
16 February 1991 – 3 February 1992	Metal Goat
1 February 2003 – 21 January 2004	Water Goat
19 February 2015 – 7 February 2016	Wood Goat

Famous Goats

Margot Fonteyn, Billie Jean King, Robert de Niro, Keith Richards, Rudolph Valentino, John Wayne, Arthur Ashe, Lech Walesa, Laurence Olivier, Mikhail Gorbachev.

Lucky Numbers

3, 4, 5, 12, 34, 45 and 54.

Character

Sensitive, altruistic and anxious, the goat is another sign that doesn't know the meaning of quitting. These are the survivors amongst us, despite the fact they often feel like giving up when the going gets tough. Goats are enduring creatures, determined and fastidious. Inventive, although impractical and lacking in foresight, goat people are likely to be well mannered and exude good taste. Respectful towards their elders and those in authority, the goat person is unlikely to rock the boat. They are conformist, docile, caring and reserved. They will listen to other people's problems be genuinely upset by the plight of others, and often find themselves stressed because of this tendency. They are not the revolutionary, but the diplomat. These easy-going people are very good at getting others to function at their best.

Goat people are not only well-behaved as children (they actually tidy their rooms) but make brilliant parents. Studious and reserved, these are people who take an interest in all sorts of subjects. Family traditions matter, and they will do all within their power to keep these alive. Even when they leave home, they will maintain strong links with the family. They can be quite nostalgic and will keep things with emotional memories, from books and furniture through to smaller objects. Emotional stability matters to the goat, and in comfortable surroundings, the goat will be quite chatty and entertaining. However, they can become pessimistic, self-centred, lazy and indecisive.

The goat is sensitive to atmospheres, and likes to have a clean and comfortable home, although it might not be tidy. Lady goats will give their all for their family, probably make their own clothes, which will be comfortable, and have many friends of both sexes. Goats will often wear things over and over again, leading their friends to think they only have one set of clothes. They just like to feel comfortable, but do like to look good, and can be very vain.

They like to please, and sometimes cook several meals at once in an attempt to make sure that everybody gets what they want to eat. However, don't criticise the end result, because goats cannot stand criticism, and you will never be invited round again. Luckily, however, they are usually excellent cooks.

Artistic and creative, these people are emotional and easily hurt. They are also easily flustered, and cope badly under pressure or when cornered. However, they will fight back if under attack.

To some people the goat may appear shy, but this is because they live in fear of upsetting others. They cannot stand the thought of being an embarrassment to themselves or anybody else. They have a brilliant sense of humour but often keep it hidden. In an argument the goat person will say nothing at all. In a crisis, the goat will be the practical person who will fetch help rather than provide it.

RELATIONSHIPS

Goat people need a lot of loving support and encouragement from close family and friends to fulfil their potential, which is great. They

are often dreamy idealists, and their family often serves to bring them back into the real world. Not likely to fall in love at first sight, the goat will be cautious and weigh up the situation before committing themselves.

The security of a stable family and homelife are essential to the goat's effective functioning. Unfortunately the goat person often doesn't know how to attract or create the stability they need. They need to feel they belong, but will not stomach even well-meaning interference.

CAREER AND MONEY

In work situations, the goat person will often find a way round a problem which other people have found defeats them and their efforts. It is not that the goat has brilliant ideas, but that he has a level of ingenuity which other signs seem unable to match, and an ability to talk people round to a more logical way of approaching the problem. Goat people prefer to work as a team, sharing decision-making, but can work well alone if necessary. They will work hard, although they hate deadlines: their only aim is to reach the highest standards. Routine, repetitive work will not be for them. They don't like to hurry things. They work well in medicine or the caring professions, and as dancers, actors, musicians and craftspeople. Showing empathy and genuinely altruistic, goat people are very generous and appealing. Their natural tact and diplomacy fits them for jobs involving arbitration, public relations, management, politics or the law. Goats are also interested in the esoteric, and may earn their living as astrologers or esoteric counsellors.

Surprisingly, goats can have terrible lapses of memory, and need reminding about appointments and time. They live in the here and now and often have little concept of the future or the need to plan. If you ask them to do something, be prepared to wait until they want to do it and for it to take a long time

HEALTH AND WELL-BEING

The goat's delicate system means they have to steer clear of exotic and spicy foods. They tend to become ill fairly easily, need lots of sleep, and hate anything too extreme.

MONKEY

DATES

2 February 1908 – 21 January 1909	Earth Monkey
20 February 1920 – 7 February 1921	Metal Monkey
6 February 1932 – 25 January 1933	Water Monkey
25 January 1944 – 12 February 1945	Wood Monkey
12 February 1956 – 30 January 1957	Fire Monkey
30 January 1968 – 16 February 1969	Earth Monkey
16 February 1980 – 4 February 1981	Metal Monkey
4 February 1992 – 22 January 1993	Water Monkey
22 January 2004 – 8 February 2005	Wood Monkey
8 February 2016 – 27 January 2017	Fire Monkey

FAMOUS MONKEYS

Michael Caine, Johnny Cash, Bjorn Borg, Ian Fleming, Tony Jacklin, Charles Dickens, Bob Marley, Peter O' Toole, Rod Stewart, Diana Ross, Mick Jagger, Elizabeth Taylor.

LUCKY NUMBERS

3, 4, 5, 7, 16, 23, 34, 45 and 54.

CHARACTER

Intelligent, obstinate, quick-tempered, easily frustrated, these are active, agile and busy people. They are adroit manipulators of circumstances and sometimes other people. They seem to be able to

talk themselves out of all difficult situations with ease. Men will try and manipulate because of job motivations, whilst women often manipulate for more emotional or personal reasons.

You can never win a war of words with a monkey: he's too clever for that. However, you can win him round by treating him to a meal with a few drinks thrown in. The monkey likes to over-indulge and he loves flattery.

Ultra-feminine, monkey women are often quite temperamental, and neither gender will stand for cross-questioning on their motives or actions. Insecure and often selfish, these people are shrewd, inventive and daring. Anything demanding thought and intrigue will interest the monkey. They are the perfect psychologists – wanting to know why all the time, needing to understand. They read up on anything new, even reading what others would class as junk mail. They also have excellent memories.

The monkey often has little time for the opinions of others. Their own opinions change with the wind, whilst their optimism remains constant. Any job which demands versatility and offers constant stimulation will interest the monkey. They often like travel, or need to change jobs or move house on a regular basis. Monkeys need new faces and new places; they abhor timetables and pigeonholes. These people are truly hyperactive, and as such get on very well with young children. Monkey people are likely to have large families.

Monkeys need support and an appreciative audience, and if they don't get these, they look elsewhere. You can spot a monkey person at a party – they move from group to group, the raconteur, telling jokes and having fun. In fact their sense of humour is the first thing most people are attracted to, and they have the great gift of being able to laugh at themselves.

RELATIONSHIPS

The monkey person will hate it if they feel they are being taken for granted, and relationships can prove problematical, with broken marriages or regular flings. They need love and understanding in the

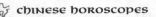 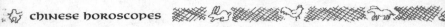

same way as everyone else, but have little patience and can be terribly self-centred. They are very intense, often promiscuous and highly sexed. They are also totally unable to show sympathy, other than by buying a present. However, they are warm, tender and compassionate when in a steady relationship.

Monkeys like to live life at speed. However, they often cause a great deal of hurt and upset because they fail to see the consequence of some of their actions, which can be terribly childish and immature. Masters of sarcasm, these people often appear arrogant and holier-than-thou. They can never understand why others should take offence at their behaviour. Monkeys view everything in a light-hearted manner, and think others should be less boring. If they do cause upset, they will appear full of remorse, only to do exactly the same thing again on a later occasion. Nothing seems to daunt the monkey – they always bounce back.

CAREER AND MONEY

Despite their nature, monkeys demand to be taken seriously, and they will react badly if you laugh at their suggestions. Don't bother offering them advice either, because they won't listen. Monkey career areas include advertising, journalism, politics, public relations, selling and driving. Many monkeys take up sporting careers, while others are entrepreneurs by day and sports players in the evening. They are also very good with figures.

Monkeys are very tempted by money, and at times this may compromise honesty and reliability. Get rich quick schemes really interest the monkey person, who is a master of sharp practice.

HEALTH AND WELL-BEING

Monkeys are normally healthy. Their only problems come through excess or burning the candle at both ends. However, their talent for self-preservation will normally see them through.

PRACTICE

We have now covered a further three animals signs. Once again, the questions below will test how much you have taken in.

- Horse people hate socialising and prefer their own company. True or false?

- Zöe was born in February 1966. What animal sign is she?

- John hates arguments. He would rather run a mile than create a problem. Is he a typical goat?

- Goat people are very family-minded. True or false?

- Monkey people rarely have problem relationships. True or false?

- Monkeys are agile and quick-thinking, and need variety and constant change. True or false?

We shall now look at the last three animal signs, the rooster (or cock), dog and pig. Once we have covered these final animals, we will be able to take a closer look at how the elements within each year affect each animal.

ROOSTER

dates

22 January	1909 –	9 February	1910	Earth Rooster
8 February	1921 – 27	January	1922	Metal Rooster
26 January	1933 – 13	February	1934	Water Rooster
13 February	1945 –	1 February	1946	Wood Rooster
31 January	1957 – 17	February	1958	Fire Rooster
17 February	1969 –	5 February	1970	Earth Rooster
5 February	1981 – 24	January	1982	Metal Rooster
23 January	1993 –	9 February	1994	Water Rooster
9 February	2005 – 28	January	2006	Wood Rooster
28 January	2017 – 15	February	2018	Fire Rooster

famous roosters

Katherine Hepburn, Richard Wagner, Joan Collins, Errol Flynn, Pete Townshend, Dolly Parton, James Mason, Bianca Jagger, Mary Quant.

lucky numbers

1, 5, 6, 12, 15, 16, 24 and 51.

character

Chinese tradition suggests that there are two types of rooster. Those born near dawn are noisy and think they are always right; those born later are quieter and less extrovert. Whatever their birth time, roosters tend to be tough, outspoken, strong-willed and active. They are self-confident and competitive, and have little patience with those who fail to meet their high standards. Artistic in the extreme, and very precise, these are perceptive people, practical and shrewd. However, they can be aggressive when threatened.

Sociable and extrovert, flamboyant yet enigmatic, roosters have a wide variety of friends and live life to the full.

Female roosters can be extremely glamorous, well dressed but

practical. Anything new or original appeals to them. They can also be difficult to live with, but that goes for both genders. Roosters excel at organising, especially parties, where they will make sure everybody has a great time. Garden parties could have a special appeal: roosters love their gardens. They seem to be able to do anything if they decide to do so, especially if it seems unusual or different.

Relationships

Stubborn, romantic, passionate and strong, these people are very attractive to the opposite sex, although they can be extremely vulnerable, and their personal lives aren't often as rewarding as they might be. They tend to be very flirtatious, and also take their partners for granted. Although highly sexed, roosters tend to think that a show of affection once a year is enough! Sentimentality is not one of their traits.

The rooster is often misunderstood, as his extreme frankness, lack of tact, subtlety and bluntness is mistaken for rudeness and conceit, and he will at such times appear downright bossy. This can sometimes be his downfall, and roosters should learn to be a little less impetuous. Roosters cannot accept criticism, and they frequently fail to listen to other people's viewpoints. Roosters take offence easily.

Rooster people are great family people, and will actively support their children in their education. The acquisition of knowledge is very important to the rooster.

Career and money

Ambitious and status-conscious, the reputation these people create matters to them, and they will work long and hard to achieve their goals, often to the detriment of their personal relationships, as they have a habit of taking on too much work. Roosters excel in careers in public relations or the media, acting (they love to dress up), teaching and entertainment. Their love of uniforms may also draw them to the military, which could also indulge their need for travel and give them a chance to wield authority. Female roosters may find themselves drawn to fashion or cosmetics, whilst television presenting or publishing will also be of interest. Both sexes will want to keep up with current fashions.

Their shrewd business sense often means that they are respected businesspeople, and their inner confidence will often carry them through times of indecision. One thing can be sure, the rooster will be fully prepared before any business meeting, and will be an effective and persuasive speaker. He is likely to have made copious notes, and will continue to jot things down as they occur to him. This person is obsessed with detail, and things must be perfect, although they hate form-filling. They are super-efficient employees, though not always punctual.

Roosters look after their money and do their homework before spending large sums, although they do indulge in occasional sprees. They like to help charitable causes when they can, and often belong to several social clubs or societies.

health and well-being

The rooster's health is usually good, although they do suffer from overindulgence problems.

DOG

犬

DATES

10 February	1910 – 29	January	1911	Metal Dog
28 January	1922 – 15	February	1923	Water Dog
14 February	1934 – 3	February	1935	Wood Dog
2 February	1946 – 21	January	1947	Fire Dog
18 February	1958 – 7	February	1959	Earth Dog
6 February	1970 – 26	January	1971	Metal Dog
25 January	982 – 12	February	1983	Water Dog
10 February	1994 – 30	January	1995	Wood Dog
29 January	2006 – 17	February	2007	Fire Dog
16 February	2018 – 4	February	2019	Earth Dog

FAMOUS DOGS

Winston Churchill, Michael Jackson, Judy Garland, David Bowie,
Madonna, Barry Manilow, Sophia Loren, Shirley MacLaine,
Sylvester Stallone, Bridgette Bardot.

LUCKY NUMBERS

1, 4, 5, 9, 10, 14, 19, 28, 30, 41, 45 and 54.

CHARACTER

The dog person is loyal, unselfish, active (though occasionally lazy),
witty, forthright and honest. These people need love and affection to
live, and are disconsolate if they feel unwanted.

They can be prone to terrible outbursts of temper, which really have
to be seen to be believed. Immediately after such an outburst,
however, they are reduced to tears and both sexes cry easily. Dog
people certainly have a loud bark, and give a nasty bite, but are
very lovable once you get to know them.

Dogs like to look after other people. They genuinely care about
those close to them, but sometimes this can make them
overprotective. They believe in fair play for everybody, irrespective
of who that person is, and will be steadfast and altruistic in standing
up for anyone in need of their support. However, don't try to

mislead a dog, as they are quick to see through attempts at deception.

Dog people are leaders, who don't take well to being led. Give them a free rein and they are happy, but tie them up and they are miserable. They thrive on responsibility, are perfectionist – even fussy, and can normally carry out even the most mundane things well. Tradition also matters to the dog, as do manners, and he will be very polite to older relatives.

Very sociable people, the dog will love to be in a group, as it gives him the chance to be the centre of attention. Dog people can, on the other hand, be quite happy in smaller groups of people, where they will sit and philosophise well into the early hours.

Dogs like sporting activities, or at least will be active in their free time. This time, however, can be limited, as these people tend to work long hours and like to work at their own pace rather than being pushed.

Dogs always think of ulterior motives when meeting others on a business footing. This can also cause them to be rather pessimistic when opportunities are placed in their court. If things turn out badly, even though to some degree this may have been expected, the dog person will handle it badly. Their normal enthusiasm will then quickly dampen, and they are probably the most vulnerable of all the animal signs to disappointments.

A tendency towards self-righteousness is one of the main downfalls of the dog person. He will worry that other people have misunderstood his motives. At such times the dog person is impossible to live with.

Serious and thoughtful, the dog can often appear to be rather condescending and hyper-critical. They can also be very judgmental, and it takes time to get to know them properly. They seem at times to live on a knife edge, and be jumpy, fractious and argumentative. At those times, it is best to leave them alone, although they won't see it that way. Seemingly never content and happy, even when things are going well for them, sometimes the dog can be very wearing on friends and family.

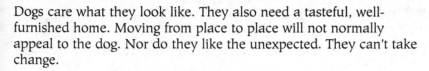

Dogs care what they look like. They also need a tasteful, well-furnished home. Moving from place to place will not normally appeal to the dog. Nor do they like the unexpected. They can't take change.

Relationships

Warm-hearted and generous to a fault, the dog will spoil friends rotten, and in a loving relationship the male dog will gladly spend a fortune taking someone out, buy roses and perfume and treat the object of his affections like royalty. If you do something for a dog person, you can expect that they will repay the debt with huge interest. These are very giving, sensitive people who fear rejection and being abandoned. These people seem to be on a journey to discover their soul mate, and they will search long and hard for that perfect person. They need to receive daily doses of tenderness and affection.

Jealousy is strong with the dog. They get very anxious about their partner's life outside of the home, and are subject to sudden changes in mood. They expect much from a partner, have very high standards, and sometimes the partner is not able to fulfil the expectations placed upon them. As a result, many dogs have more than one marriage, and many remain single. Dogs make good parents, doting yet strict, they are very loving.

If the dog takes a dislike to you, no amount of trying will change his opinion. Once decided, the dog's mind is fixed. People who are friends with the dog will be friends for ever, and as a result his large circle of friends very rarely gets a lot of new blood introduced. Anybody who interferes or invades their private space will find themselves particularly unwelcome. Dogs do have secrets, although to many acquaintances this would seem unlikely.

Career and Money

Careers for the dog person include anything involving people, from sales and marketing through to the caring professions. Working in the law also will appeal, as will anything involving teaching or the armed services. All dogs have a deep sense of duty. They also have a deep interest in anything paranormal or mysterious, and as such

may practice astrology or tarot, or be deeply interested in spirituality or reincarnation.

Great employees, these people like to be involved. The dog demands to be treated fairly, and if given responsibility, will work long and hard to achieve results. Money doesn't necessarily matter that much to the dog, although he will expect fair remuneration. These people are not materialistic, but more idealistic. Cautious but successful in business, they are popular bosses, treating their employees well, and being diplomatic where conflict could occur.

health and well-being

Health problems don't crop up too often for dog people, other than nervous problems, which can beset them at any time, especially if their home life is unsettled. They rarely suffer from anything serious, and older dogs often seem younger than their years. They may suffer back problems, and they often suffer with arthritis as they age. It is lucky for the dog that they fall ill so rarely, as dealing with illness is not one of their strong points. They should try to worry less.

Dog people love open spaces and will find recreation and relaxation in the countryside. They will often walk for hours. Anything remote and wild will appeal to the dog person, and as a result, many dog people take mini-breaks in the Scottish highlands, the Peak District or the Lakes in England.

ᴅᴀᴛᴇꜱ

30 January	1911 –	17 February 1912	Metal Pig
16 February	1923 –	4 February 1924	Water Pig
4 February	1935 –	23 January 1936	Wood Pig
22 January	1947 –	9 February 1948	Fire Pig
8 February	1959 –	27 January 1960	Earth Pig
27 January	1971 –	14 February 1972	Metal Pig
13 February	1983 –	1 February 1984	Water Pig
31 January	1995 –	18 February 1996	Wood Pig
18 February	2007 –	6 February 2008	Fire Pig
23 January	2012 –	9 February 2013	Earth Pig

ꜰᴀᴍᴏᴜꜱ ᴘɪɢꜱ

Tennessee Williams, Johnny Mathis, Maria Callas, Henry Ford, Humphrey Bogart, James Cagney, Ronald Reagan, Jean Harlow, Elton John, Jerry Lee Lewis.

ʟᴜᴄᴋʏ ɴᴜᴍʙᴇʀꜱ

1, 3, 4, 5, 8, 16, 18, 34, 41 and 48.

ᴄһᴀʀᴀᴄᴛᴇʀ

Tolerant of other people's failings, sincere, easy-going and placid, honest, loving, creative, good company, generous to friends, these sincerely nice people are homely sorts, who will take time to listen to someone's problems and give sound advice. They are open-hearted and respect their fellow beings, but also respect themselves. Pigs can often seem just too nice, but don't tell them, because they won't be able to understand that at all!

Fond of their food and drink and prone to excesses of both, the pig also ends up taking on too much of other people's problems, and then will be nervous, tired and grumpy. Pigs make brilliant arbitrators or intermediaries, but should watch business lunches and dinners, as they really do eat too much.

Flirtatious and charming, these cool customers have a need to speak the truth, but can be very secretive when it suits their purpose. They

rarely reveal all their cards at one time. Practical and sensible, they know what they want, where they are going, and ultimately how to get there.

Pigs can be very stubborn and 'pig-headed' at times, and whilst they may listen to advice, they will invariably make their own decisions. Sometimes they are just over-confident.

Making an enemy of a pig is a big mistake. They make few enemies, because they like to get on with other people, and will offer people lots of chances, but when someone crosses them or is deceitful towards them, they are prone to awesome rages. When crossed, the pig is hot-tempered, and not above making snide and abrasive comments. These rages, which match anything other animals can dish out, can normally be abated by feeding the pig or by offering an expensive malt whisky. He will normally cool down when food or drink comes his way. Pigs don't like arguments anyway. They will normally state their case, and then get out. That's on the assumption that they face up to the situation in first place. Pigs will do all they can to avoid confrontation, sometimes deliberately changing the subject.

These people are very protective of themselves and won't be pushed by others, however well-meaning they might be. Never meddle in the pig's secret or personal life. You will surely ruin the friendship, and live to regret it.

Pigs respond well to flattery, and are often duped by someone who knows how to flatter them and tell them how clever they are, or how lovely they look. Pigs love clothes, and tend to dress up, especially on special occasions. Being beautifully turned out is a must for both male and female pigs, and they will tend to go for striking colour combinations.

These people are country and garden lovers, interested in history and tradition, and likely to be quite conservative in thought. Manners matter to the pig, and they are masters of good taste. They are also easily impressed by 'names', famous people or those who have made it to the top of their profession.

Pigs tend to worry if they think they have done something immoral

or unwise, and wrongdoing of any kind will make them extremely nervous. In their personal lives they tend to trust other people too much, and a good actor or actress with a well prepared story can easily con the unsuspecting pig. Despite this sensitivity, the pig will rarely worry what other people think.

Fun-loving, chatty and well read, the pig has strong passions, and they show, even though they may think they are skilfully concealed. They cannot hide their emotions, as their facial expressions give them away every time. Unlikely to stay in the doldrums for long, the pig will cheer up himself and everybody in his immediate circle, and face the next set of challenges with renewed faith and confidence. Pig people are nearly always cheerful.

The pig is forever on the go, is industrious and works hard, commanding the respect of fellow workers, but will always take time out when hungry (which is nearly always), or when there is a need to lend somebody a hand. Should you find yourself without a bed for the night, you can be sure your pig friend will put you up and feed you. If the roles were reversed, that is how the pig would expect to be treated, although to be fair the pig rarely asks for help, probably because they hate to be indebted.

Few other animals work as hard or as long as does the pig, but when work has finished, his equally active social life may cause him to become over-tired and withdrawn. Whilst they love company, they don't particularly like huge crowds, especially if there are lots of people there they don't know. They feel more comfortable with hand-chosen guests.

Their home life will always matter to them. They love their families and are practical around the house. Pigs like a clean, orderly and tidy sty, and their homes are normally quite pristine – although sometimes, just to prove a point maybe, the pig home is really untidy. Pigs either love housework or hate it with a passion.

Pigs are good talkers and listeners, and enjoy gossip, but getting a pig involved in a debate can be a difficult task. The pig likes to take time to think about his or her involvement in outside issues. Yet once involved in a debate, the pig can be very forthright, although

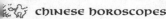 
pigs sometimes fail to check their facts adequately, and are known to exaggerate or enlarge upon the truth.

Relationships

Loyal, honest and faithful, the sensual pig loves with passion and intensity. Pigs tend to fall in love with ease, and they tend to fall head first. Most pigs have several romances before settling down, and are very popular with the opposite sex, although they can be very possessive and exceptionally jealous. Romantic and idealistic, these people try hard to remain sensible and earthy, and not let themselves fly off into flights of fantasy too often, although in the initial stages of attraction, pigs will spend ages staring into space, thinking about the object of their desire.

Pigs will do anything to please their partner, and nobody will be left unaware of the fact that the pig is in love. Open displays of emotion come thick and fast. If rejected, or should a relationship sour, the pig will throw him or herself into work, leaving little time for thinking about the past or for a new social life. However, when asked about his last love, the pig will visibly relive the whole affair, and can be quite disconsolate. If in a stable relationship, however, the pig will want to talk about it all the time.

It takes time for a pig to make a move on a prospective partner, and they prefer to get to know someone first, most likely in a group situation, before feeling comfortable about going on a one-to-one date. Sometimes they wait too long and miss the opportunity – to their lasting regret.

Career and Money

Pig people often overspend on meals out, drinking sprees and holidays, but their workaholic tendencies usually provide the money to pay for these indulgences. Pig people often become rich, and are often determined to stay at the top of their profession. They have a talent for making money, and for keeping it. They are born collectors, and often collect things which will appreciate in value.

Good careers for the pig will include any job which puts them in the

limelight or offers the chance to entertain and receive applause. They work well in theatre, films and TV. These are cultural people, and they will normally be very musical or at least appreciative of fine music. The pig is also good at charity fundraising, and anything involving a charity should be considered. Good at troubleshooting for a business, they work well with others. They also make excellent business people, provided they can live outside the city.

Female pigs often give up any idea of a career upon marriage and arrival of a family, and so there are only a few famous pig ladies.

health aNd well-beINg

Pigs suffer badly from stress-related problems, often of their own making.

PRACTICE

We have now covered all 12 animal signs, and can start to think of the elements, and how these affect the essential characteristics of each animal. Before you move on, try the questions below to see how much you have understood and remembered.

- Dog people will run a mile from an argument. True or false?

- Roosters are survivors. They always bounce back. Can the same be said for the dog or the pig?

- Dick was born in January 1969. Is he a rooster?

- Dog people are always looking for their soul mate, and are probably interested in reincarnation. True or false?

- Pig people hate admiration, and anything which places them centre-stage will be detested. True or false?

- Dogs and pigs are both likely to be prolific charity workers. True or false?

3 ThE ElEMENTS

A ll the animal signs have now been covered, and whilst we have mentioned the elements associated with each year, we have not as yet discussed how this affects each animal. In this chapter we are going to look at the elements sign by sign, and see how they alter the characteristics we have already discussed.

The years for each animal are also given, but make sure to look back at the full dates as given earlier, as only the years, rather than days and months are given here, so January/February birthday people need to check.

ThE RAT

METAL RAT ~ 1900, 1960

Cultured and refined, this very competitive yet loyal person will have a lovely home and appreciate the finer things in life. Likely to cultivate friends who mix in the best circles, this person is likely to be emotionally insecure, and appear cold and calculating, but is sure to be on a sound financial footing. Metal rats need to succeed, and can often be very materialistic. This is the all or nothing person, who dislikes sentimentality and uses other people and situations to their own ends. They should try to curb their ruthless streak and be less aggressive and judgmental. Their tendency to use others as stepping stones to the top can alienate them from many individuals. Metal rats use their charm, vibrant enthusiasm and brilliant chat-up lines in the pursuit of wealth, and few signs are more serious in their intentions towards greatness or guarding of their reputation once they get there.

WATER RAT ~ 1912, 1972

This person is a thinker, someone deep and astute, who is popular and friendly but fears being alone. Charming and quiet, this rat loves to travel and gets on well with other people, being tactful and diplomatic. Journalism would be a good career for this person, as he is clear-thinking and expresses himself well, as would anything involving diplomacy or fashion. These people have a sweet tooth and like to live in comfort, if not luxury, often forgetting the other side of the coin. Loyal and sincere, the water rat can be rather lazy and expect others to carry too much of the workload. Emotionally, this person needs someone strong and courageous to balance them and keep them optimistic for the future. These rats have a tendency towards self-pity and are easily duped.

WOOD RAT ~ 1924, 1984

Artistic, caring and romantic, these people are sensitive to surroundings and love the countryside. They are at their most creative in the evenings. Although friendly and outgoing, they are unlikely to have a huge circle of friends. They are rather insecure but their sense of humour usually sees them through. They often appear totally carefree, although they do worry, especially about their family. They can do most things well, although they need to be told often and loudly how capable they are. Unlike other members of the rat group, they relax with ease. Career areas include art and writing.

FIRE RAT ~ 1936, 1996

Witty, forthright but sensitive to criticism, these people are prone to over-excitability, and can be easily unsettled. Full of energy, they never sit still and won't be hemmed in by anybody or anything. Independent and impatient, these rats need new situations and new challenges on a daily basis. Charming and sensitive, they are very careful with money, and often make lots of it. These rats hate their own company, and need to be with other people to be happy. Stoical and honest themselves, they need their friends to be loyal and truthful.

 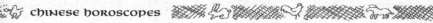

earth rat - 1948, 2008

Earth rats are level-headed, practical, resourceful and cautious. No-nonsense traditionalists, they want to get to the top in their career and frequently do. These people can be disciplined and hardworking, yet often appear self-satisfied and self-righteous. They are caring and generous family people, romantic and affectionate, who often worry unnecessarily about other people's views of them, but are normally very successful. They can be demanding. Great at throwing dinner parties, these people can be very judgmental, and yet find no problem in extramarital affairs. Good parents, the earth rat's progeny are likely to be well turned out, nicely spoken and sociable.

The ox

metal ox - 1901, 1961

Tactless, blunt, forthright and determined, this person can be his or her worst enemy because of their attitude – they seem unable to take into account the fact that other people also have the right to their opinions, and often appear grumpy. Unlikely to let you down once a promise has been made, this person will have hand-picked friends, will be difficult to live with, have lots of drive and be very dependable. Metal oxen ooze charisma but are likely to hypercritical, moody and unable to accept any criticism themselves. They are nostalgic and sentimental. They should learn to watch their jealous and possessive nature when it comes to matters of the heart.

water ox - 1913, 1973

A better team-player than most of the ox family, this person is an organiser, was probably a studious pupil who enjoyed working to a routine, and enjoys working for humanity, often for charitable causes, especially to do with the environment or nature. Not likely to be party people, they bide their time, weigh up the pros and cons, and then act quickly, often surprising other people by the swiftness

of their actions. Like most ox people, they insist on doing things their way. Popular and friendly, this person is unlikely to be deceived by others, and will have a calm and gentle approach, but often succeed in getting things done while others are still trying. The water ox can be very suspicious in romantic matters. Family-minded, the water ox expects much from his family, and can be very loving and caring, but a touch inflexible. Don't upset them, however, because water oxen can be real tyrants when the mood takes them.

WOOD OX - 1925, 1985

Imaginative and practical, these confident people work well alone and will stick to any task undertaken. Unhappy when idle, they have to be doing something, whether it is working, reading or studying. They like to lead, will give their all, but have quick tempers if things don't go according to plan. Like the elephant, these people never forget. They need to have everything their way, and will do anything in their power to make sure that is the case, from being downright domineering to being very generous in order to win people round. They are humorous, chatty and great company, but they abandon those they see as rivals or who disagree with their ideas. For this reason, they are not very popular, although they try hard in this respect. They are devoted family people and often have large families, even if it is by several relationships. They will happily move home for the sake of their family. They survive, no matter what.

FIRE OX - 1937, 1997

Sharp, assertive, conscientious, active, keen-witted, strong in body and mind, these people fall in love easily, but their love is often unrequited. They aren't subtle at all, and can be very impatient and egotistical. These people have hand-chosen friends, are devoted family people, who have a tangible sense of responsibility, and are kind and generous to their loved ones, although their sense of empathy is negligible. They often go far in their career, probably because they plan well in advance for every eventuality, and have the ox's inherent belief that they are always right. Hardworking and capable, these people will give their all for the things which they consider right and true.

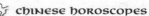 

EARTh OX ~ 1949, 2009

Sensible, logical, sincere, tactless, ambitious and shrewd, good judges of character and respected business people, the earth ox is likely to be the person friends turn to for help and advice, although they rarely have a stable emotional life themselves, being rather naive. Interested in other people, and their business, they have a tendency to tell other people what to do all the time, and have strict rules of conduct and behaviour. They have huge appetites, and their partners know that they can be won round by a huge meal, well prepared, followed by a sensual display of affection afterwards. Earth ox people are very sensual, but likely to be unromantic. Self-centred and believing in total perfection in all things tackled, they are practical people, reliable and hardworking. In love, they often fear rejection, can be very insecure, and are likely to appear aggressive as a result.

The Tiger

Metal Tiger ~ 1890, 1950

Ambitious, outgoing, assertive and impatient, these are hardworking people who expect things to go their way, and thrive when there is an element of competition. Respected and admired, this person is never short of a goal to aim at, and success is of paramount importance. Full of energy and drive, this is the person who often puts on a mask to hide his or her feelings, as they find it very hard to show themselves for all to see, even in close relationships. Likely to be sharp-tongued and sometimes lacking in understanding in emotional situations, these tigers need to be a little less bossy and realise that other people have the right to voice their opinions, even if they differ from that of the metal tiger.

Water Tiger ~ 1902, 1962

Quite a motherly, loving type, irrespective of gender, this person is likely to want to travel far and wide, and probably retire early to foreign climes, where they can indulge their love of foreign

languages. These tigers like to entertain and be centre-stage, and often find themselves drawn to careers in the entertainment or teaching fields. Able to handle stress, fair-minded, clear-thinking and likely to have lots of interests, this is the ambitious and persuasive person who gets what he or she wants and succeeds in business. Creative and imaginative, these people are very versatile, but not always faithful in their relationships. Good careers would include anything in entertainment, teaching, law or languages. They need to watch their tempers, which flare up dramatically at times. They make formidable enemies.

WOOD TIGER - 1914, 1974

Pleasant, intense, passionate and romantic, these people are very creative and artistic, and look to others for help more often than other tigers do. Active and witty, this person probably has several jobs at the same time. Appearing hyperactive and unable to switch off, this tiger loves and needs change and constant stimulation. They are full of great new schemes and ideas, and they assume everybody and everything will fit in with them. Unlikely to settle down without feeling trapped, wood tigers need a lot of time to do their own thing, and while they may fly into tantrums at times, they will quickly forget and get on with life. Sociable and friendly, this tiger reacts well to flattery, and is a boon at a party.

FIRE TIGER - 1926, 1986

Magnetic, generous, optimistic, charming and passionate, these people dislike criticism and cannot take advice under any circumstances. This tiger can be ruthless in business and emotional matters, and will not suffer fools gladly. Even more energetic than the other tigers, these people often burn the candle at both ends, and their drive will not diminish until they are forced to slow down. Enthusiastic and imaginative, they like to lead, and are eloquent speakers, who should watch their nerves and the speed at which they work and play. Stoic, determined and quite innovative, this tiger is unlikely to marry young, being far too involved in career matters and needing to get to the top before looking for a partner.

earth tiger - 1938, 1998

This is the specialist within the tiger group, the permanently well-dressed, dependable person who takes on one thing at a time and sticks with it. Loyal, passionate, jealous and possessive with family and friends, this person prefers to lead. They are independent, restless, ruthless and stubborn. This person will rarely admit to any failings, or to being wrong. Unlikely to listen to advice, although actively courting it, the impatient earth tiger is nevertheless friendly and well liked, and usually offers good advice which they should perhaps listen to themselves! Many earth tigers take up jobs in politics, because they feel the need to fight for the underdog and against injustice.

The RABBIT

metal rabbit - 1951, 2011

Calm, loyal and quiet on the surface, but ambitious, capable and shrewd underneath, this person sets about getting to the top at an early age, and is very strong-willed, even aggressive. Protective and defensive with family and friends, they are very possessive, but their word is their bond, and they never let people down. Likely to be interested in the arts, in anything esoteric or mysterious, these people can use situations to their own advantage, but can often have too high an opinion of their capabilities and be far too serious. As a result, these rabbits seldom have a large circle of friends and are unlikely to share their thoughts with anybody. Metal rabbits are somewhat depressive at times, and think things through slowly and carefully.

water rabbit - 1903, 1963

Sensitive, intuitive and quiet, these people have long memories and never forget a hurt. They are artists, dreamers and idealists who are rather squeamish and hate horror films. Education will have featured prominently in their lives, and they are very well read, great conversationalists on all sorts of subjects, and likely to accumulate

much wealth. Family life matters to the water rabbit, and they are romantic and loving people, who are likely to be well respected in their career. Their homes matter to them, and they are very clean, tidy and orderly, although their health can be rather delicate.

WOOD RABBIT - 1915, 1975

Considerate, sociable, likeable, generous, affectionate, easy-going and kind, wood rabbits are brilliant with children, older people and the sick. Often seen as the proverbial good samaritan, these people beaver away, dislike any upset and often need strong partners. They will try to ignore people and things that cause waves for them, as they need a peaceful environment. Wood rabbits dislike being centre-stage, but working back-stage could suit them, as they expect things to be done properly, and are very organised. Totally lacking in romance, the wood rabbit is unlikely to buy flowers, cards or presents for his or her loved one.

FIRE RABBIT - 1927, 1987

These people excel in the fields of medicine and the arts, being naturally intuitive and charming. Enjoying reading, these people have good memories, and work involving administration or the government might also be of interest to them. They are enthusiastic, friendly, outgoing and sometimes over-confident people who need a challenging career. They work hard, often forestalling problems, but they also play hard, and can be very self-centred, especially when it comes to matters of the heart. They are likely to have more than one marriage. With the correct help, these people go far, although too much stress can make them moody and temperamental, and they often suffer with nervous problems.

EARTH RABBIT - 1939, 1999

The earth rabbit doesn't say a lot, but misses nothing, and can usually persuade other people to their way of thinking. They work long and hard and are usually good in business, being naturally thrifty and cautious, and definitely speak their minds. Reliable friends and colleagues, these people are greatly respected, listen to

advice, but can be terribly critical of others and upset people with their attitude. They need the security of a permanent relationship in order to thrive, and will find themselves naturally interested in reincarnation.

ThE ÐRAGON

METAL ÐRAGON - 1940, 2000

Blunt, often to the point of tactlessness, this is a terribly ambitious, hard-working, optimistic and energetic person, who keeps going along his path in his way, and will either succeed or fail abysmally, this sometimes being caused by involvement in things which are a little devious or dark. Metal dragons like challenges. Banking, politics and international affairs are suitable career areas for them. They are well liked and respected, and are forceful and ambitious types, although they like to do everything by the book. A tendency towards jealousy can often sour emotional relationships, and they should watch their awful tempers and guard against taking too many risks. Likely to be interested in comparative religious studies, also in collecting information, this person would make a good researcher or journalist, and could find themselves marrying for money rather than for love.

WATER ÐRAGON - 1952, 2012

Friendly, understanding, caring, intelligent and humorous, this person is the originator of the 'one liner', and is often an effective and eloquent speaker or writer. They are frequently intuitive and interested in mysticism, yet they also read everything factual they can lay their hands on, and will remember where they read it if asked. They love a challenge, especially if it involves an element of mystery. Water dragons seize opportunities. Being naturally creative, the water dragon lives for love, and in romance is likely to seek a soul mate. They care about their friends' well-being, and like to be involved in as much as possible with them. They will ring them often, and help them out when needed, or just provide a shoulder to cry on. They also love to hear all the news, being very curious and

inquisitive. They want to know all there is to know about everything, including how it works and why. These people always have several jobs, can turn their hands to anything from writing to performing, are amusing, sociable people, but sometimes mean with money. They are animal lovers.

WOOD DRAGON - 1904, 1964

Creative, bold, witty, inquisitive, unconventional, generous, warm and loving, these people aren't always very practical, but have great vision and ideas. This dragon really is a deep thinker, who sometimes thinks on totally abstract lines. Another who acts quickly, this person is quite diplomatic for a dragon. Responsibility sits well with wood dragons, and they are always there for friends and family alike. Mediation is one of their strong points, and they make excellent diplomats and counsellors. Active both in work and outside, these dragons can work in any field, from education to art. Philosophical and non-confrontational, they love discussions and will talk long into the night if given the chance.

FIRE DRAGON - 1916, 1976

Eccentric, ambitious, conscientious, strong-willed, stimulating and adventurous, these people love to spend money, and how! Not fond of group settings, these are creative and artistic people who often fail to take into account the views of others. Born leaders, these dragons work hard in all their endeavours, but are often unapproachable and superior in attitude. That said, at least they will accept that they can and do make mistakes. They are great partners and friends, can be very generous and giving, but can also be very vindictive and hard. Give them a large project to work at and they will be happy.

EARTH DRAGON - 1928, 1988

The quieter dragon, this is the reflective person who needs praise but is capable, organised and clear-minded. Money is not the be all and end all for this dragon, but they do need a career which allows them to be centre-stage and gives them the freedom to move about at will. Romantic and imaginative, and likely to have a lot of friends,

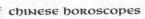 
the flamboyant and extrovert earth dragon will always find help for his or her projects and often succeeds in obtaining huge wealth. Genuinely wanting to help other people, they will not be compromised over matters close to their hearts. Quite eccentric (as are all dragons in degrees), this person needs to have a partner to love and look after, even if they find fidelity a bit of a problem.

The snake

Metal snake ~ 1941, 2001

Determined and independent, ambitious and often successful, the metal snake needs security, and is unlikely to take many risks, although they rarely miss a good opportunity to add to their finances, and can suffer from delusions of grandeur. Wary of opposition in business, and needing people on their own wavelength, this person doesn't share feelings in words, but is very open in actions, and will be interested in art and music. To the outsider, this snake will appear cold and distant. It is just that this private snake doesn't trust strangers, and their naivity can cause problems for them. Often attracted to the wrong people, and likely to need more than one partner, this person is very intuitive and self-confident.

Water snake ~ 1953, 2013

Studious, quietly spoken, well-dressed, reserved and capable of assimilating a lot of information, water snakes often specialise. Possible careers include law, science and the media. These are loyal snakes, who are deep, imaginative and profound thinkers, and are often attracted to astrology or psychic work. They need partners who think along the same lines, who appreciate nature and won't let them down. They also need someone who lives life for the now, rather than the future or the past, but above all someone who is honest. These snakes aren't into flings or affairs – they are too decent for all that!

wood snake - 1905, 1965

Anything mysterious or intricate appeals to these people, who have
many love affairs, which often end in upset. Careers in acting, public
speaking, or communications are very good bets for the pleasure-
seeking wood snake. Anything which allows them to make and then
spend money, indulge themselves and win the approval of others is
a must. Witty and interested in the arts, these are the people who
give out advice to others but often need it themselves. Jealous and
possessive, the wood snake expects a partner to be with them
constantly and often allows them no freedom. Friendly and needing
lots of company, this snake will hate his or her own company in a
big way.

fire snake - 1917, 1977

Elegant and refined, these people are often the partner of someone
exceptionally successful – the power behind the throne. They can be
very forceful and ambitious and are likely to travel far and wide.
Whilst they are happy for their partner to be in the public eye, you
can bet that they will be on that publicity photograph themselves
somewhere. Their public image will matter a lot to them, and they
won't do anything which could sour their reputation. Likely to use
other people in their rise to power, these snakes are good company
and will help friends whenever they can. Careers in politics, acting,
travel, film or television are likely to prove of interest. Secretive but
loving, these people have great taste, but often upset others by their
need to voice their opinions.

earth snake - 1929, 1989

The earth element exercises a calming and practical influence, and
the earth snake is likely to be sensible, thorough, organised and
stubborn, although somewhat of a dreamer, who doesn't always see
things through. A true survivor, this snake will work hard but won't
like anything too rough or manual. Give them something to sort out,
however, and they'll be more at home. Good with money, this
likeable person will help the family at no matter what cost, but can

irritate by being so precise and unfeeling. The earth snake can be very devious, a plotter and a downright liar when it suits, and needs a stable home environment with as much luxury as possible.

the horse

metal horse - 1930, 1990

These people like things to happen quickly, and need to develop patience and the ability to work to routine. Popular, very well dressed, demonstrative and highly intuitive, they can be rather self-centred, and hate people who interfere in their lives. Good business people, needing money and status, they fear nothing, and positively welcome confrontations. Optimistic and friendly, the metal horse is very attractive to the opposite sex, who will find them exciting and dashing. These are the swashbuckling, bold, confident and ambitious sorts, who see themselves as heroes rescuing those in distress. They may marry for reasons other than love, and often keep a very tight rein on their emotions, fearing being hurt more than most horses.

water horse - 1942, 2002

Water horses like to mix with the best. If they can't, they will at least have a good try, and given even half an opportunity, will grasp it and move forward. Loving change, sports and travel, these restless people also like to dish the dirt, and will know all there is to know about everything, or think they do. Liking to travel and needing constant change, they have problems with relationships, are self-centred and easily bored with routine, and need to work at this long and hard if they are to be successful. Those who marry a water horse should be prepared to move house regularly. Their sense of humour often carries them through, and they are brilliant conversationalists. They are generous and kind, but need to be boss, both at home and at work.

wood horse - 1954, 2014

Fair-minded, agreeable, determined to succeed, these horse people are very artistic and somewhat workaholic, with an almost tangible sense of duty. Romantic, innovative, caring, thoughtful and loving, these people are good friends and provide sparkling company. Despite this, they have a problem with relationships, and can be very opinionated and feel themselves superior or at least different to everyone else. Impatient and yet co-operative, the wood horse will not be led and will need to be active all the time. These people are great at self-promotion, but are very critical of others at times. City life is not for this horse: they are country folk through and through, but they still need a busy social life.

fire horse - 1966, 2026

Fire horses are clever, able, active, strong-willed and sporty. All or nothing people, they are the icing on the cake among the animal signs. Complex and exceptionally difficult to understand, they are ruthless people who often fail to see their own vulnerabilities, becoming downright objectionable. Their love to travel will lead them to move about a lot, and they often fail to reach their goals because they can't settle down. They are romantic, magnetic, flamboyant, inconsistent, and dreadfully strict as parents, and they rarely fail in any endeavour. Unable to share emotions, rather aloof and unsympathetic, selfish, funny, creative, loving, they are true revolutionaries, who are blunt and forthright and need to make their mark.

earth horse - 1918, 1978

Financial security matters to these people. They are brilliant in any form of self-employment because they work long and hard, and have good business acumen, but their emotional life is often flawed, and they are very indecisive and bossy. They can be wise and perceptive, but they can be fickle and cynical about matters of the heart. Music will always be an interest to an earth horse, and they would do well to include it in their career. These people dislike jobs that are too

serious or bound by routine. They are charming, caring, witty and considerate to friends, but slightly more hostile towards those outside their circle.

The GOAT

METAL GOAT - 1931, 1991

Anxiety lies just beneath the surface of this seemingly calm and composed person. Not the sort to have arguments, the metal goat's easy-going nature is often exploited. Things go at a very slow pace for the metal goat. He won't like rushing about or making snap decisions. Good in business and likely to have money put by for a rainy day, these are demanding people, especially in relationships. Loyal and conscientious, this person probably hoards things, but is likely to have an orderly house. Casual dress rather than formal attire is the rule with the metal goat. They have an excellent way with people, and make great psychologists, social workers, actors and socialites. They should try to keep their ambitions contained, for fear of becoming too carried away.

WATER GOAT - 1943, 2003

Popular and witty, this modest person lacks confidence and often needs encouragement. Communication comes easily to these goats, and they thrive when given a chance to show how well they write or draw. These people are note-takers, and are very likely to keep diaries of their day-to-day activities, not for any reason other than the fact that they cannot share secrets with other people. Security matters, and the water goat won't take risks or adapt easily to change. Instinctive and sensitive, the water goat is a charming and tactile person, who often needs a bit of a push and can be very self-effacing.

WOOD GOAT - 1955, 2015

Quiet types, these thoughtful people are gentle, trusting and kind.

Likely to have a large family, and feel the need to please everybody all the time, wood goats are very artistic and will have a genuine love of nature and children. Acting is a profession suited to these people, as is anything involving teaching. Slightly more bold than other goats, this person seems always to be smiling and happy, but is really quite moody. Only those close to the wood goat see the depressive side of their character. When in a down mood, music or dancing should generally cheer them up. They are great dancers.

fire goat - 1907, 1967

Persistent, charming, persuasive, diplomatic, patient and helpful, these are the teachers within the goat group, and should also consider jobs in medicine, health or philosophy. Though great at parties, this person isn't too brilliant at budgeting, and has a vivid imagination. Money may be a constant problem for the fire goat. This goat loves to spend money, often failing to make sure that the cheque they have just written will be met. Living on credit is a terrible temptation for them, and they should keep a close watch on their credit card statements. Passionate and vital, this is the person who is up one minute and down the next, and likely to give up on a project when the going gets a little tough. Anything out of the ordinary appeals to the fire goat, and they are very interested in anything esoteric.

earth goat - 1919, 1979

Loyal, sensible, caring, compassionate and studious, this goat has no concept of saving at all. Money is to be spent, and especially lavished on family and friends. Reliable, sociable, friendly and hard-working, this goat is a good employee, but they should be left to go their own way, as they won't like being told. Problems with relationships tend to happen because they are rather blunt, but that is basically because they fail to think a lot of the time, and aren't very logical. Although erratic and temperamental, these goats make good listeners, and will try to understand, whatever the problem.

The monkey

metal monkey - 1920, 1980

Extrovert, strong-willed, passionate and romantic, these people are all action, but not within a team framework – they are better in some form of self-employment where they can travel about, sales work being particularly well suited to their needs. Not afraid to work hard, and likely to plan their finances, they are secretive and cautious people, who deep down are very insecure and frequently depressed. Witty and good fun, the metal monkey is often jealous and possessive. Possible careers include the arts and media, but medicine would also be a good choice, as would financial speculation. Unfortunately, they tend to spend such a lot of time on their career that their personal life suffers. They need someone who is independent and understands the monkey's need for freedom for the relationship to succeed. The metal monkey won't spend much time at home!

water monkey - 1932, 1992

Good company, versatile, perceptive, understanding and level-headed, these people make brilliant investments for the future, don't mind taking chances and work well with other people, provided they aren't put under too much pressure or criticised. They need plenty of change, variety and travel. Possible careers include teaching, nursing and the armed forces. Romantic and loving, these monkeys are homely sorts who get on with most people, but they can be very restless and need a lot of tender loving care. They are witty and attentive, passionate and serious in matters of the heart, but can be highly strung and tend to think that they have upset people. Easily manipulated by stronger people, the water monkey is very good at solving other people's problems, but not their own.

wood monkey - 1944, 2004

Cautious with strangers to the extreme, obstinate and set in their

ways, these people are also efficient and methodical. Enthusiastic and imaginative, they notice their surroundings and like to learn new things. They are loving and caring, and often pick partners who are stronger than themselves. They have terrible tempers, are highly creative and inventive, and tend to enlarge upon the truth. Good career options include marketing, public relations, journalism, legal work or anything which allows them to travel. Long-term relationships are really not their scene, although they do try very hard. Sometimes their partners just can't stand the pace. These people really want to be somebody, will study for ever and probably reach the top through contacts rather than through hard work.

FIRE MONKEY - 1956, 2016

These people are terribly analytical and will weigh up others to the nth degree. They can be very headstrong and focused at times, but are loving and passionate to their family. These are the leaders amongst the monkey group, who thrive on creating mischief, and expect people to see their point of view. Sporty, unpredictable, competitive, clumsy and creative, they are always on the go, and need to learn to relax a little, before they burn themselves out. Good career choices are anything sports-related or which allows them to be creative, working well behind the scenes. They also love anything which allows them to enter into debate. Honest, imaginative and idealistic, the fire monkey works hard, plays hard, and pays the consquences.

EARTH MONKEY - 1968, 2028

Another homely sort of monkey, these people hate change and can become very bitter when things don't go their way. Genuinely caring about other people, they value education and place great importance on things being perfect, including their relationships and their home. Impatient and self-reliant, they work well on their own, are often suspicious of other people and don't therefore work well in team situations or let other people into their confidence. Studious and quiet, these people often accumulate a lot of money for their retirement, but also have fun, especially with romantic encounters.

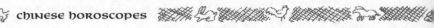

Careers could include outdoor jobs. Mobile catering is a strong choice, as is anything which allows them to help the less fortunate. These people are brilliant organisers, have a huge helping of common sense, and usually live to a good age.

The ROOSTER

METAL ROOSTER - 1921, 1981

This person knows at an early age what they want, and will go for it, believing they know best. Very organised, these are the people who need to be tidy and will carry this through by tidying up other people's homes when they visit. Loyal and friendly, but often too aggressive, this person likes to have a challenge and to be in a competitive situation, and will work well for charity groups, also being attracted to work in the public eye, in politics, theatre, film, television or the media. Metal roosters can be very temperamental at times, especially in relationships, where they can be downright bombastic and overly candid.

WATER ROOSTER - 1933, 1993

Eloquent, understanding and helpful, the water rooster loves debates and discussions. A natural worrier, with a huge inferiority complex but also a great sense of humour, this person gets on well with others and usually gets to the top of his or her profession. A balanced and happy personal life is important to this rooster, who will love to sit back at the end of the day and listen to soothing music surrounded by their family. These people don't like to be alone, and yet lose friends because they are unable to accept any help or advice. Great salespeople, the water rooster also makes a good teacher.

WOOD ROOSTER - 1945, 2005

These people can pick up anybody's sullen mood and turn it into happiness. Creative and full of life, they are team players, who often demand much of their partners, and are passionate, considerate,

caring and yet headstrong. Wood roosters need a lot of attentive love and affection, and need to be told they are wanted and needed. Tending to bounce from project to project, they need to learn to tackle one thing at a time. Very conscientious and able, the wood rooster is a good friend and companion who will think of him or herself as a perennial Peter Pan, dressing in a youthful way and keeping up with current musical trends.

FIRE ROOSTER - 1957, 2017

Romantic but not successful in love, these people seem to live on a knife edge all the time, and outsiders wonder if they go round looking for arguments. Strong-willed in the extreme, they are efficient people who tend to steamroller less forthright people in their group. Though not always as successful as they should be, fire roosters are great organisers and hard workers who never let disappointments prey on their minds. Popular and fashion-conscious, they are also likely to be very intellectual. They are tactless, nonconformist, sentimental, and easily won over by tales of gloom and doom. Complex and difficult to understand, the fire rooster has probably the most volatile emotional life possible.

EARTH ROOSTER - 1909, 1969

Perceptive and intuitive, these people succeed in business because they stick to their course. For similar reasons, they tend to marry late in life, as they know what they want from a partner, and will wait until that person comes along. Loving and caring, the earth rooster will hate demonstrative shows of affection, but will always be there for their family. Likely to be interested in the arts, and probably quite theatrical, the earth rooster works long and hard and is organised, well liked and respected. Family will also matter, and they are supportive and caring parents. They may make successful careers in banking, management, accountancy or research, as details and order are important to them.

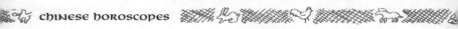

The Dog

Metal Dog - 1910, 1970

Intuitive and spiritual, these are the dogs who seem forever torn between materialism and philosophical pursuits. They are very curious, and can quickly become defensive if they feel threatened. Leadership matters to the bold metal dog, and he will be organised and careful in his choices. Difficult and obstinate, critical and outspoken, they have problems with relationships and often live alone, throwing themselves into their work or a charitable cause. They take some getting to know but are loyal and caring. They speak their minds and never give up on something that matters to them, but they like to see a little recognition at the end of it all. Career choices could include the police and research.

Water Dog - 1922, 1982

Anxious and often pessimistic, these dogs are active and enterprising, fair-minded and honest. They will stick at something for ever, like the proverbial dog with a bone. They often lack self-confidence, despite their self-assured, direct and outgoing façade, and will often seek, and follow, advice from friends and family. They need to express their feelings, and they demand loyalty. Aggressive, analytical and aloof, this person is very sensitive and caring, and is difficult to get to know. The water dog spends money easily, and is likely to move around a fair bit, in search of the perfect place. Blessed with good memories, these people are great friends, rarely make enemies, and will help in any situation, even if it means personal sacrifices.

Wood Dog - 1934, 1994

Practical and capable, these people love gardening and home improvements. Highly intuitive, this is a dog with a loud bark, which isn't always prefaced by a growl. Often turning to food for comfort,

these dogs appear cool, calm and collected on the surface, but are often very nervous underneath. Affectionate and loving, they are able to identify deceit and deception with ease, are loyal and gentle, with a dry sense of humour. They never stray far from their home environment, work well in group situations, love the countryside and hearth, and are truly charming people who like the finer things in life. Sometimes too altruistic and sensitive, the wood dog makes a great champion of charitable causes.

fire dog - 1946, 2006

Alert and engaging, intelligent and active, these people thrive on hard work. Although sometimes hyperactive, they often find themselves in a deep depression, and their idealism may cause them problems. They are honest and outgoing people, but they are also demanding and can stifle their partners by being over-protective and at times aggressive. They are certainly not easy to live with, and can sulk for days when things aren't going well for them. They are unlikely to spend much time at home. Career choices could include mediator, trouble-shooter, counsellor and critic. Passionate, friendly, stubborn, vital, belligerent and awkward, these people are also interested in anything remotely mystic, new or different. Their main problem is that they cannot see they could be wrong in anything.

earth dog - 1958, 2018

Analytical and conservative, though generous and devoted, these people are very astute and money-oriented. They need to be recognised in their career, and are likely to use others to their own ends. They trust nobody, and can be very authoritarian and bossy in approach, so they may work better alone. The earth dog is quiet, realistic, cautious and sceptical, and not at all romantic. Over-eating is one of their main problems, combined with nervous problems due to stress and tension. Possible careers include banking, teaching, property development and politics, as they are very persuasive types, methodical, creative and efficient. These dogs are good parents and loving friends. Family and relationships will always come before career for these dogs.

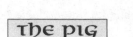

The PIG

Metal pig ~ 1911, 1971, 2031

Obstinate and often in an awful hurry, these people are charm personified, although they may have an elevated opinion of themselves and an ego to match. Determined and trustworthy, these are energetic people who will always try to improve on their achievements. This pig will not readily strive for fame and fortune. They won't be too propelled by money, although they can acquire a taste for it, and will likely have been pushed and cajoled to the top by someone slightly more ambitious. They will have lots of interests and probably more than one job. Property speculation will appeal, and the metal pig may move around a lot on their rise to the top. Trusting in the extreme, these friendly, warm people have a lot of friends, but normally take a long time to settle on their choice of partner, and as a result may marry late in life. They are likely to be fairly strict with themselves, but they will run a mile from conflict.

Water pig ~ 1923, 1983

Artistic and communicative in their professional capacity, shy and retiring with people they don't know, these pigs are very shrewd and persistent. Making probably the best diplomats of the pig group, these are clever and versatile people who flourish in the world of travel or sales. Fond of children and very caring and affectionate, these people value personal happiness above monetary considerations. They enjoy having lots of people they know around them as they like to share conversation and talk over the day with someone on a regular basis. This pig is likely to enjoy food and live in quiet luxury, while knowing how to save the pennies! Trusting, loyal and worried in case they make waves for anybody else, these are quiet types who work hard and like outdoor activities. They are also brilliant in fashion and design, being naturally well turned out themselves, and make great charity workers.

WOOD PIG - 1935, 1995

These people do well in business, advertising and public relations. They are witty and know how to make other people see their viewpoint, but unfortunately they fall foul of the well-spun yarn. Caring, friendly, loyal, optimistic and home-loving, these people will do anything to help their family, friends or environment. They need to be involved in everything, and often take on too much. They have a problem saying no, and are often too kind-hearted and soft for their own good. They let other people upset them far too much, and can then sink into quite a depression. One problem for this pig is that they find it difficult to show their emotions when in romantic situations, and as a result can need a lot of encouragement and tender loving care. They enjoy music, reading and art.

FIRE PIG - 1947, 2007

Even-tempered, energetic, adventurous, confident and strong-willed, nothing will seem to bother these pigs, but they should learn how to be patient. Again, fashion, media, publicity and marketing are their forte. A great person for following causes and championing the underdog, these pigs are very stubborn once they have made up their mind about something or somebody. They are born entertainers, loving and generous family people and amusing friends. The family is vital to the fire pig, and they can often be very pushy but loving parents, whilst being unable to push themselves. Fire pigs should learn to be a little more flexible in opinion, and should widen their horizons, their viewpoints and their circle of friends.

EARTH PIG - 1959, 2019

Hard-working, even-tempered, sensible, realistic, practical and able, these are the people to have on your side if you have just started up a business. They will take it to the top, or die trying. It is as if they need to impress, but it would be useless asking this pig why he does things, as he is likely to be the very last to know, or to understand.

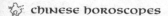 

They are skilled persuaders, and generally get the best from others. They could do well in medicine, as they really know how to be innovative in the science field. They are also likely to have an interest in the past, and as such many earth pigs work in archaeology or antiques, and in museums. They have quite a refined palate, but they should learn to watch what and how much they eat, as they really are comfort eaters. Another animal who won't like living in a city, this pig is quite innocent and vulnerable, and can be easily duped. Lacking in sophistication, these people are blunt and likely to put their foot in it.

pRACTICE

We have now covered all the elements associated with each individual animal. Before we move on, however, we must again test our knowledge and understanding.

- What are the five elements associated with the animal signs?

- Generally speaking, what does the earth element bring to each animal sign?

- Which animals discussed in this chapter would be best suited to working in the medical profession?

- Do metal ox people work long and hard to attain their goals?

- Does the metal pig person need a push to get to the top?

- Would a water dragon be a good public relations person?

4 THE YEARS

*W*e have now learnt about the animal signs, the elements and their meanings. We now need to look towards the future, and what the animal years traditionally hold in store for each sign.

As we know, the first animal sign is the rat, and we are going to start by looking at a rat year, and work through each animal sign to see whether its years, as a general rule, are good years. It is also possible to look at national and international trends for each year, but we will only do this briefly here, as we are out to discover more about ourselves and our friends rather than about political situations.

THE RAT YEARS

1900, 1912, 1924, 1936, 1948, 1960, 1972, 1984, 1996, 2008

A time when secrets are revealed, both personally and internationally. This is also a year when friends tend to help those in need and when a general feeling of well-being develops. As this is the first of the animal signs, a rat year traditionally signifies the start of new things and the growth of new ideas, and is a good year for opportunists and gamblers. As with anything new, projects don't really grow to their full potential this year, but the foundations are being laid. A good time to utilise talents and potential and get going. Rats years are important, as what happens during this year has wider implications for future years.

The Rat Year by Sign

Rat   A great year for rats, who really get going in career and personal matters. Things go really well this year, but it is not a time to rest on your laurels. Plan, work hard, but enjoy yourself.

Ox   A chance to get going is offered, and you should take it. Lots of opportunities in career and romance, although not for starting new romantic attachments. This is a good year for holidays and a brilliant year for sorting out problems, as you feel quite benevolent.

Tiger   Not a great year for the tiger, this is a year when it is best to keep working on what you already have and maintain a reasonably low profile. Risks are best left during the rat year, and it is better to save rather than spend.

Rabbit   Rabbits shouldn't take chances this year, and others may be deceitful and want to trip you up. A year when things just won't go according to plan, when losses may occur, and when it is best to avoid speculation.

Dragon   A good year, especially for money matters. Things are on the up and up during the rat year. Love flourishes, and you feel generally very happy with your lot. Watch your spending this year, as you may need extra funds in the future.

Snake   A good year financially, but not for stress-related problems. The snake should invest money and watch it grow during a rat year. Ups and downs are on the cards for the snake this year, but overall things will go well.

Horse   A year when the horse's heart really isn't fully behind his undertakings, this year really can be quite difficult. Money may be needed for large items, and spending should be watched. This is not the time to make demands.

Goat   Plan, save and invest wisely during the rat year. Try to guard against spending on anything other than complete necessities. This will not be a year for fun and leisure, but for work and planning.

Monkey   A great year when everything financial comes up trumps. Things seem to go well for the monkey during a rat year, but

 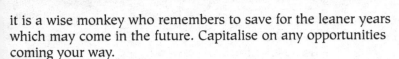

it is a wise monkey who remembers to save for the leaner years which may come in the future. Capitalise on any opportunities coming your way.

Rooster   A mediocre year, when thoughts should be on saving for the future, making wise moves and not doing anything rash, which will be a big temptation. This is not a year for gambles, and roosters should watch their emotions.

Dog   A year to cruise along and keep going, rather than making sweeping changes or altering course. Rat years are far too materialistic for dogs. Don't give up though. Better things are round the corner.

Pig   A great year. Things go really well, providing that you keep to the chosen track, don't slacken off, and don't deviate. Socially, things are really on the up, and invitations are likely to come in thick and fast. Romance is especially well starred.

The Ox Years

1901, 1913, 1925, 1937, 1949, 1961, 1973, 1985, 1997, 2009

Years when it is necessary to consolidate and wait. Not a time for new things, but a great time of those prepared to work hard. This is a time of stability and comfort stemming from previous ideas and actions, and a time when good judgments are made. Traditionally a good year for marriages (which consolidate the engagement), things work well in this year only if sufficient forethought has gone into their preparation.

The Ox Year by Sign

Rat   Not a great year. Keep your nose to the grindstone and work hard, even if you don't feel like it. Give late nights a miss and concentrate on work this year.

Ox   A year when you might feel out of it all at work, but a good year for home and family. Plan for the future now, decide where you want to be and what is needed for you to get there, and do something about it.

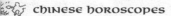 

Tiger   All work and little play, this year means you are likely to feel very frustrated about things. There may be problems connected with contracts, and you should watch your temper.

Rabbit   Extra burdens may be placed on the rabbit this year, and it would be easy to quit. Don't make any decisions which could affect your long-term future. Wait a while.

Dragon   A mixed year when you may find criticism hits home, and you should really try to maintain a low profile. A good year financially, but you must watch temper outbursts.

Snake   Knuckle down to some hard work this year. This is not a year for plans but for getting down to it. Quite a hard year but a good one if you keep going.

Horse   A great year for the hard-working horse, and one when you can enjoy yourself, with no money problems. Career advancements are likely, although romance isn't so well aspected.

Goat   Not a happy year for the goat. Pressures at work will cause disruption to your routine. This is a work year with little outside activities to balance it out.

Monkey   Be prepared to work long hours, or find someone else who can do it for you. A slow sort of year, so use the time to get healthy and fit for the years to come.

Rooster   A better year than the last, when money matters improve and things finally seem to be working. Romance is still a little problematical, maybe due to your approach?

Dog   A year when you might be wondering where you are going. Sit back and try not to worry about it all. Not a year for new ideas or anything innovative. Try not to rock the boat.

Pig   A reasonable year, but not one when you finally 'get somewhere', even though you work exceptionally hard and have no time at all for relaxation.

The Tiger Years

1902, 1914, 1926, 1938, 1950, 1962, 1974, 1986, 1998, 2010

Action years, sometimes really turbulent, when things really come to the surface, whether good or bad, and can change quickly and dramatically. Tiger years are traditionally fairly hard on the emotions, and demand courage. Good years for the self-motivated or naturally intuitive, bringing huge gains for some people and huge losses for others.

The Tiger Year by Sign

Rat   Not a bad year, but many changes will occur around and about you, which may upset your sense of security. Keep going, take stock of the situation and relax a little.

Ox   Maybe the pace this year is too fast for you. The only way is to ride out the storm in the safety of the things you know.

Tiger   A brilliant year, with tons of get up and go and lots of things going well. This could be your year, especially for romance and love, and in fact it could be your decade if you start to plan properly now for the future.

Rabbit   Taking a calculated risk could pay off this year. Start the year slowly and then rise to the occasion. Lots of chances to make money, but watch partnerships.

Dragon   A great year. Go for it with every ounce of determination you can muster. Make the most of each and every opportunity, but don't get conceited.

Snake   A year of opportunities to take or dismiss, as you see fit. There'll be lots of action, but maybe it will be a bit too much for you!

Horse   You are likely to have a good time this year, with lots of challenge and prospects for investment. Lots of action and lots of chances to shine.

Goat   You may find this a difficult year, as things aren't going your

way. Just keep going and don't make waves. It pays this year to develop patience – remember, it's a virtue!

Monkey   Not a bad year for you, but watch you don't get carried away with schemes and plans, and beware of complacency which can cause you problems. People from the past often reappear during this year.

Rooster   A turbulent year, and one when spending is likely to get out of hand. A lot of changes tend to make you feel uncomfortable, but you have to go with the flow regardless.

Dog   This year, you might finally get the recognition you deserve for the altruistic way you handle yourself. A good year, when people listen to you, but do be careful when it comes to signing anything legal. A good year for romantic attachments.

Pig   Not a bad year. You will find things relatively easy this year, but you won't make a fortune. There will be change in store this year, and you could find yourself on the move.

THE RABBIT YEARS

1903, 1915, 1927, 1939, 1951, 1963, 1975, 1987, 1999, 2011

A year for moderation in all things. This is a time when peace talks stand a good chance of succeeding, or on a more personal front, when long-standing arguments and rifts can be healed, and peace and harmony can rein. Steady progress is normally made this year and past efforts rewarded. As the rabbit is a quiet sort of chap, this is not the year to rant and rave, as nothing will be achieved. Families are important during rabbit years and tradition suggests it is a good year in which to buy property if you wish to speculate.

THE RABBIT YEAR BY SIGN

Rat   A pretty spartan year. You must set your house in order, and you won't like that. A year when you should keep a relatively low profile, as there are many misunderstandings and confusions this year. A good year to think about further education, this is a year which could be fairly good for business.

 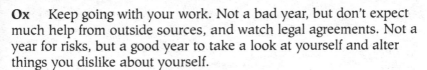

Ox   Keep going with your work. Not a bad year, but don't expect much help from outside sources, and watch legal agreements. Not a year for risks, but a good year to take a look at yourself and alter things you dislike about yourself.

Tiger   A year when you must dot the i's and cross the t's and that will make you feel a little uncomfortable, as detail isn't your forte. People will notice you more this year, and you should take a look at your overall image and rectify things which need to change.

Rabbit   A good year for you. Things go well, and this could be your year, if you allow it to happen. Romance could be better this year. Keep an eye on money matters and take a few risks.

Dragon   A pretty OK sort of year, with chances to get attention and push new ideas forward, but on the whole a quiet time, when you could start to think about hobbies a little rather than work.

Snake   A good year for you to make your mark. Stop hiding your light under a bushel and shine. A great year for romance. More money around this year too! You'll be busy all round.

Horse   A reasonable year, workwise, but not so for the homefront, where you could find yourself bored rigid. Don't let it get you down.

Goat   A great year. Lots of opportunities, lots of happiness, and finally you feel that you are turning the corner towards the sort of life you want to have. Parties, invitations and lots of friends. What else can you ask for! At times you may feel a little down, but not for long.

Monkey   Not a bad year. If you have plans, give them an airing this year, and also look at where you want to go. Other people may help you in your plans.

Rooster   A year when you realise that the only person likely to help you is yourself. A good year for work but not for romance.

Dog   Not a bad year really. Personal difficulties may occur during this year, but you can cope with all the ups and downs. Friends will be there for you, and long-standing relationships are favoured. Not a year to try to shine. Work in the background.

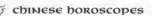 

Pig   A good year for family and home, but there may be problems on the workfront to deal with, and confrontation may be necessary, with the correct professional advice being sought. Not a bad year though, if you are aware that others may be looking to trip you up.

The dragon years

1904, 1916, 1928, 1940, 1952, 1964, 1976, 1988, 2000

Lots of opportunities abound during the dragon year, as it is a year of possibilities, good for partnerships and anything unusual.

Impulsiveness, characteristic of the dragon, will also be a part of this year, and new ideas and energy will move people to do things they would not normally think of undertaking. Things which seemed impossible in the rabbit year will now be easier to conquer for those who wish to take the chance. Another year when things go very well, or terribly badly, often making this the year of what might have been.

The dragon year by sign

Rat   Opportunities abound this year. Lots of money to be made, so get out there, and romance isn't too far behind. It is possible that investments will pay dividends for the rat this year. There are lots of social events to entertain you. You will probably spend a lot.

Ox   A year of hard work and little time for play. You should work at your own pace rather than allowing others to force the issue, and plan for the future.

Tiger   A creative year for the tiger, and maybe a good year to settle down, but not a year to push yourself too far into the limelight. Keep on track and maintain a low profile.

Rabbit   Not a good year for the rabbit. The pace is too quick and the rabbit won't feel comfortable. A good time for family concerns, concentrate on your home life this year.

Dragon   This is your year to act. Your career goes well and personal life blooms. Use any spare time to plan for the future and where you want to be in a couple of years' time.

Snake   Chances to make quick money may present themselves. On the whole, though, a pretty quiet year, and one when you should try to remain in the background where possible.

Horse   Too much to do this year means you are likely to take a back seat for a while. A good year for romantic commitment, and a great year for parties and social activities.

Goat   A reasonable year, with the emphasis on money and planning for the future. Try not to overspend.

Monkey   A good year financially with plenty of chances for financial security. Don't be tempted to overspend, even though you feel you can afford it.

Rooster   A great year in store for the rooster. Plans and ideas prove lucrative. A good year for partnerships, both personal and business, this year will be one to remember.

Dog   Not a great year. Worries and anxieties are likely to surface, and you may feel like you are swimming against the tide. Listen to other people and try to be less gloomy.

Pig   Lots of work to do, lots of money to be made, but little chance for recognition. You could end the year feeling decidedly uneasy.

The snake years

1905, 1917, 1929, 1941, 1953, 1965, 1977, 1989, 2001

A deceptive year when things aren't what they seem to be, but also a year when it is possible to turn the tables and reverse previous trends. A good time to look closely at your individual motives, snake years bring the need to wait to see the actions of others before acting yourself. A good year for partnerships, although these are likely to be unorthodox.

The snake year by sign

Rat   Passion and romance are very likely for the rat this year, but things may not go according to plan. Problems are likely in the

workplace, and money will be tight due to last year's spending. Conserve whatever money you have for the future.

Ox   A year when you might be forced to slow down and reflect on the state of things. Keep saving whenever you can. Romance is likely this year, but watch your health.

Tiger   Just when you think you're getting somewhere, maybe you find you aren't, other than in the romance market, which flourishes with a passion this year. The pace will be slower than you would like in business, and this could cause you problems.

Rabbit   A peaceful year, with lots of friends and get-togethers, but don't let other people's problems upset your own equilibrium. You should end the year with more money than at the start.

Dragon   Success and happiness this year, even if the pace is a little less frantic than you would wish. Work hard and keep at it, and be careful with business plans. A good year for anything creative or musical.

Snake   A happy year when things are just right for you. Romance is especially favoured, whether you already have a partner or are seeking that special someone.

Horse   Things happily tick along, with or without your help. You may find it all rather boring and lacking in excitement, and your love life could be better. Plan for the future.

Goat   A great year with lots of social opportunities and chances to shine, especially if you are involved in artistic or creative things. Lots of romance will keep you busy!

Monkey   There are some good chances to earn extra money during this year, but probably away from centre-stage. Watch your temper, slow down a little, and take life a little more seriously. Passion levels run high for you this year!

Rooster   A good year for business and pleasure, but there are likely to be things to deal with which you won't like. You need to face up to things this year and deal with them now. Romance may be strained.

Dog   Expect people to take notice of your plans this year. A good year for you, but don't push for the limelight yet. Not a good year to ask for a loan. Try to watch your spending.

Pig   Romance may hit hard this year, and you will be so wrapped up with it all that you may fail to work as hard at work as you would normally. Watch your emotions, as this year you could get hurt. A year of turmoil really for the heart.

The horse years

1906, 1918, 1930, 1942, 1954, 1966, 1978, 1990, 2002

Routine work flourishes during the horse year, as this is a time when energy levels are likely to be high for the majority of signs. Not a time for changes, in a horse year it is best to build on what you already have, or wait until a better time before starting something new. A need for honesty is paramount during these years, as history has shown more skeletons to come out of cupboards during horse years than others. Fire horse years (1966 for example) are very turbulent. Horse years are normally very romantic and passionate.

The horse year by sign

Rat   Not a good year at all for the rat. Overspending is very likely and social events won't go well at all. You will feel totally out of sorts for the majority of this miserable year, and business prospects aren't good, either.

Ox   A year of work for you, but you are prepared to work long and hard, so this shouldn't be too bad. Other people may steal your limelight, but only if you let them.

Tiger   You are likely to have a bit of extra cash this year, but will probably spend it on your love life, which will blossom. Keep plodding on at work, and don't take gambles or burn the candle at both ends.

Rabbit   A busy year, especially socially. Remember to conserve energy levels. Maybe you should review your commitment to various projects.

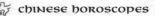 

Dragon   A year when fate can take your future one way or another. Keep going along your path, don't make waves, and it will be all right.

Snake   Extra hours at work are likely to be asked of you during the horse year, which means less time spent on personal pursuits. You will probably feel misunderstood fairly frequently. Don't let it affect you.

Horse   Likely to be a really good year for you, or conversely a really bad one, and not a particularly brilliant year for the other animals. Things are likely to change, and you shouldn't consider any long-term commitments during 'your year' because it's all too unpredictable.

Goat   A reasonable year for you with lots of social activities and rewards for work undertaken. Gambles and speculations could pay off, but do try to stay backstage for a while.

Monkey   Confrontations are likely for the monkey this year, but you'll get by. Opportunities are there if you look for them.

Rooster   A year when you can finally clear up any debts, have a bit of fun, and end on a positive note. Not a year for huge speculative ventures, it is a great year to take a look at yourself and rectify any faults you find.

Dog   You could find yourself puzzled by affairs of the heart, because other people don't understand your motives, and you may wonder where you are going. Not a bad year for finances, but try to be less analytical and stop blaming yourself when things go wrong.

Pig   Be careful with your love life this year. Last year was a little hard on the emotions, but this year flirting is likely to bring you problems, and it could all get a bit serious.

The Goat Years

1907, 1919, 1931, 1943, 1955, 1967, 1979, 1991, 2003

A stocktaking year when the future can be planned, and generally a good year for those in authority, or those working for the benefit of

mankind in medical research or pioneering techniques. A good year also for marriages and settling down, but not too brilliant for those wishing to end a relationship. Goat years are generally a good time for the fashion industry to create startling new looks. People seem to be able to get away with not pulling their weight this year – bosses please note!

the goat year by sign

Rat Time to kick off the dust and get on with it. The past is gone and the future is there before you. Lots of opportunities but take care how much you involve yourself with, as you can find yourself over-committed, and end up without anything to show for the effort.

Ox Never one for a wild social life, this year is best left to its own devices as far as the ox is concerned. Not a good year for you, try to avoid stress and tension, and relax as much as possible.

Tiger You can have too much of a good thing, tiger, and by the middle of the year, all these activities will begin to lose their appeal. Not a great year, and again you'd do best to maintain a low profile.

Rabbit A good year for you, but one when you should try to liven up your social life, but still try to make time for your own relaxation. Don't overload friendships by demanding unnecessary attention.

Dragon This will only be a good year if you are involved in artistic pursuits, in which case you could really get to the top. Otherwise nobody seems interested in any of your projects or plans.

Snake A good year for creative projects, but not for romance or anything involving the welfare of other people. Money may be short at times.

Horse A year when you should stick to what you know best, but should find things go well all told. Romance is especially well aspected, and marriage could be especially successful.

Goat A great year for money, career and romance. Lots of chances to have good times. Everything will seem to go your way. Enjoy it!

Monkey   Could be a costly year for you, but you will have a good time. Lots of ideas and lots of things to do, when people will ask for your opinion and listen to your advice.

Rooster   Why do all the bills seem to be addressed to you this year? You won't be too happy about all this. Maybe you should have saved for this year! Other worries will take up your time, but only if you let them.

Dog   Lots of parties, but maybe you won't feel like them. Get your sleep, stay inside and do your own thing. A good year for anything creative and for learning new skills.

Pig   A great year for social events, but you can't be in two places at the same time, so choose wisely. If you've been feeling a little unsure, this year will clear your path. Go for it.

The monkey years

1908, 1920, 1932, 1944, 1956, 1968, 1980, 1992, 2004

A year of contradiction and uncertainty, when it is easy to make terrible mistakes, and leap from the frying pan into the fire. Those who are into speculative ventures can make fortunes in the monkey year if they buy and sell quickly enough. New and unusual things happen during this year. Most people have a good year, with plenty of laughs along the way.

The monkey year by sign

Rat   Quite a good year. You could make a bit of money this year, rat. Use your natural talents, and sort out the wheat from the chaff. Love is also in the air, and you could find that special someone this year.

Ox   Not a good year for the ox, but one when offers may present themselves, and you could do well if you want to. Too much fun and not enough work being done all round you make you tense and irritable.

Tiger   A reasonable year, with lots to do and people willing to help and listen to your plans and ideas, but you could feel that you are

bashing your head against a brick wall. Not a year for partnerships.

Rabbit   At time when a bit of risk-taking might pay off. Things could work out well, but the outcome is uncertain. Probably better to go underground this year!

Dragon   A good year, if you plan things properly and look before you leap. Lots of money likely, bargains to be had, but not a lot of praise from other people. Romance is well starred.

Snake   You will end the year with more money than at the start, but it will be hard graft which will win through, not easy opportunities. Keep your temper and back off.

Horse   People might try to trip you up this year over financial deals. Not a good year for romance either. Be especially careful this year, as there's a lot of deceit about.

Goat   Tradition suggests this is the best year for the goat to marry. However, watch the pennies, and don't make any hasty decisions. Think things through properly.

Monkey   This is the year you really come out on top. Nothing can stop you, people seem to love you to pieces, and you are in great form. Money isn't as tight as it was, and you should sort out financial commitments if possible. Plan for the future.

Rooster   Keep working hard, and it will eventually pay off. Don't get involved in other people's problems and disagreements. They are none of your concern. Stay with what you know this year.

Dog   Things can tend to go downhill a little after a promising start. Maintain your realism. Money prospects will improve, and you may have opportunities to change your lot.

Pig   A great year for lovers, this is also a good year for new ideas and for making money, and you will have more than your fair share of love and money this year. Traditionally this is a year of make or break.

The ROOSTER years

1909, 1921, 1933, 1945, 1957, 1969, 1981, 1993, 2005

Often difficult years, those people who want to make a real impact in their career can often do so during a rooster year. People seem to be generally more helpful during a rooster year, but it is also a time when independence reaches a high point, and relationships can easily flounder. This is a time when hard work really pays off, but when those out to trick or deceive fall flat. A good year for challenges and changes of any description, the rooster year often brings about an element of peace, but all signs must be flexible.

The ROOSTER year BY SIGN

Rat   A satisfactory year for the rat, despite the fact that there isn't much money around. You may be criticised over your behaviour a little more often, and you should watch your roving eye in romantic matters.

Ox   A great year for you, with people seeming to be genuinely interested in you and your plans. Lots of money comes your way, but beware of double dealing. Opportunities to diversify or push for the top should be seriously considered.

Tiger   A feeling of restlessness this year, when you may wish to move. Keep working and don't give up. Relationships go well, in fact better than for some time.

Rabbit   You work at your usual pace, but feel left behind. Money doesn't come when expected and you may find yourself with extra bills. Curtail your spending a little and dig in!

Dragon   One of the best years financially for the dragon. Lots of praise and applause at work, but perhaps a little more romance wouldn't come amiss. Those already involved may find they hit a few problems this year.

Snake   Not a bad year in all probability for the snake, in romance and in business. Lots of hard work, but few quick rewards at the end of the day. Maybe next year!

Horse   Lots of rich pickings around for the horse this year, but things may not be very clear. Perhaps a change of job should be considered, or even better a change in lifestyle.

Goat   A year when all those skeletons may come crashing out of the cupboard. Not a bad year though, all told, but one when you may feel you are swimming against the tide.

Monkey   Do be careful in partnership matters this year. Generally a good year financially, but try to think more about your family, who need some attention.

Rooster   Money comes to you this year, but it could be tough at times. However, a good year for you, and you should plan for the future, and avoid overspending.

Dog   If you remember to keep going when things don't seem too good, you will end the year on top. It isn't that important for everybody to agree with you all the time. A year for treading water, keeping going and saving money.

Pig   Romance and business both go well this year, but guard against overspending. Traditionally this is the best year for the pig to marry. Make the most of the quiet times.

THE DOG YEARS

1910, 1922, 1934, 1946, 1958, 1970, 1982, 1994, 2006

A time to guard against the future, it is better to be honest in a dog year, save money rather than speculate, and avoid risk-taking. Probably the best year in which to marry. Relationships cemented during a dog year are traditionally based on trust and deep devotion, which are the dog's main character traits.

THE DOG YEAR BY SIGN

Rat   A good year for business, but a poor year in the romance stakes, when there will be a fair bit of tension and disruption. Not a good idea to get engaged or married this year, as your level of tolerance is at an all-time low, and making promises now is not a good idea.

Ox   Things don't go according to plan this year, so it's probably better for you just to plod on. Take a holiday if you can.

Tiger   A good year, if you remember not to push too hard, or too soon. Lots of romance for you to enjoy this year, and you will feel on cloud nine.

Rabbit   Keep going and you will be fine. A reasonable time to speculate or invest for the future. Don't worry so much about everything.

Dragon   Money matters go well this year, and it is a good time to consider going it on your own. If you remember to do the best for yourself as well as for others, you will do well, but not without a lot of hard work and change. Do temper your flirtatious side!

Snake   Things go at a steady tempo, with nothing too pacy. Lots of opportunities, but watch your health and stop worrying. A bit of relaxation wouldn't go amiss.

Horse   A reasonable year, but not a time to think about yourself too much. Think about other people and try to help them when you have the chance. You will benefit from it.

Goat   Not your year at all. All talk and no action leaves you feeling down and totally ignored. A year for quiet contemplation maybe.

Monkey   You win some, and you lose some. This year is one of those years for you, as people and situations let you down. Keep working at it and don't let your spirits be dampened.

Rooster   Not your sort of year. Be careful what you do, as you can so easily upset everybody this year. You really need to work hard to re-establish what may have been lost last year.

Dog   A great year for you, when all the worries and troubles you've experienced pale into insignificance. People will listen to your ideas and you really can't go far wrong. You might even be able to sit back and relax a while.

Pig   Honesty really does pay dividends for you now. A good year for business, but a better year closer to home.

The Pig years

1911, 1923, 1935, 1947, 1971, 1983, 1995, 2007

Things aren't always what they seem during a pig year, as it can be a time of illusion, with a lot of unnoticed things going on behind the scenes. A good year for investigations of any sort, it is a time to tie up loose ends, being the final year in the cycle. This also means it is a year when past actions or efforts will either be rewarded or rebound. It is often a time of prosperity. Reflective and thoughtful years, pig years can often see the culmination of hard work and effort or conversely be a time to make decisions about the future. Traditionally, pig years are times of wealth and happiness.

The pig year by sign

Rat   A good year for the opportunistic rat. Maybe you should think about helping some less fortunate members of the animal family. Socially a great time, with lots of scope to enjoy yourself to the utmost.

Ox   People will help you if you ask. Hard work and effort will pay off for you, although your health could suffer from overwork. You may suddenly start to move forward.

Tiger   A good year for you. Lots of ideas and many of them will be taken up by other people, earning you lots of praise. Money could be tight, so try to pull in the reins especially where family and friends are concerned.

Rabbit   A year of love and happiness for you, in huge portions. Chances to make money are around, and you will end the year with a healthy bank balance and maybe extra inches around the waist!

Dragon   Extra money comes your way this year, and you may meet someone special, or at the very least, win someone over to your way of thinking. Everything seems, finally, to be going your way, but don't get carried away.

Snake   No money problems for you either this year, but there may be catches. Think about how you want to spend your cash, but don't make rash decisions.

Horse   Money and romance for you this year. This could be the time for settling down and trying to reduce your high stress levels by taking time out for a change.

Goat   You will love to spend money this year, and be very happy as a result. Watch your diet. Relax and avoid stressful situations.

Monkey   Lots of social gatherings, but do watch what you say, and to whom. You can easily trip yourself up with your tongue this year. Gambles may pay off, but tension surrounds you.

Rooster   A happy year when you feel you can join the party, rather than staying on the outside. Romance is likely to hit a few rocks this year, but financially things will be fine.

Dog   A good year for you again. You can show the kind and compassionate side of your nature, and you won't feel too compelled to work all the time. A good year for property purchase and holidays.

Pig   A great year for you. Make it one to remember. Think about settling down or start a new business, but do plan for the future. Money and help come to you this year from varying sources, including from someone who thinks a lot of you.

PRACTICE

Now it is time to test your knowledge. Try your hand at the questions below.

- Who does best in a dog year?

- How would you, as a pig, expect a pig year to go for you?

- You are a rooster. It is dragon year. What is your best course of action this year?

- How would you expect an ox to fare in a tiger year?

5 COMPATIBILITY

We have now looked at the future, but how do the 12 animals get on together? When thinking in terms of compatibilities, we normally think about romance and love. However, there are lots of other interactions, such as business, and we should also look at this before we can really say we have begun to understand the complexities of Chinese horoscopes.

Before we get too involved with each of the animals, let's take a quick look at the elements, which you will recall we discussed in detail in Chapter 3.

In the table below, which is fairly general, you will see how the elements relate, male and female. The key to understanding this is that 1 is great, 2 is good, 3 is perhaps a little more difficult, 4 is likely to be problematical and 5 is better left alone.

	Female Wood	Female Fire	Female Earth	Female Metal	Female Water
Male Wood	5	3	1	3	2
Male Fire	3	3	2	4	5
Male Earth	5	2	2	1	4
Male Metal	3	5	4	5	1
Male Water	2	5	4	1	3

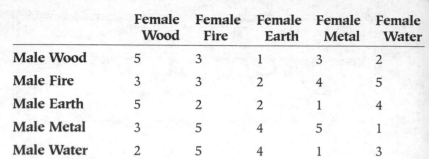

	Female Wood	Female Fire	Female Earth	Female Metal	Female Water
Male Wood	5	3	1	3	2
Male Fire	3	3	2	4	5
Male Earth	5	2	2	1	4
Male Metal	3	5	4	5	1
Male Water	2	5	4	1	3

Bear this in mind as we now take a look at the signs, as we will not be dealing further with the elements in this section. The following charts have exactly the same key as that given above (repeated from the previous page). We will deal with each animal individually, starting with business relationships and then looking at the love angle.

Each chart rates the prospects for relationships between the sign in the heading and the signs listed. For example, a rat – ox business relationship scores 4.

RAT

	Business	Love
Rat	5	1
Ox	4	3
Tiger	3	4
Rabbit	2	4
Dragon	1	2
Snake	4	3
Horse	5	4
Goat	4	5
Monkey	3	2
Rooster	5	5
Dog	4	3
Pig	3	3

OX

	Business	Love
Rat	4	3
Ox	4	4
Tiger	5	5
Rabbit	3	3
Dragon	5	4
Snake	5	4
Horse	2	4
Goat	5	5
Monkey	5	3
Rooster	3	2
Dog	5	3
Pig	2	2

TIGER

	Business	Love
Rat	3	4
Ox	5	5
Tiger	5	5
Rabbit	3	4
Dragon	1	1
Snake	5	5
Horse	2	2
Goat	4	3
Monkey	4	4
Rooster	5	4
Dog	5	4
Pig	3	3

RABBIT

	Business	Love
Rat	2	4
Ox	3	3
Tiger	3	4
Rabbit	1	2
Dragon	2	1
Snake	2	3
Horse	2	2
Goat	2	2
Monkey	5	3
Rooster	4	5
Dog	3	4
Pig	2	3

DRAGON

	Business	Love
Rat	1	2
Ox	5	4
Tiger	1	1
Rabbit	2	1
Dragon	4	5
Snake	3	1
Horse	2	3
Goat	3	2
Monkey	1	1
Rooster	1	3
Dog	5	5
Pig	1	2

SNAKE

	Business	Love
Rat	4	3
Ox	5	4
Tiger	5	5
Rabbit	2	3
Dragon	3	1
Snake	5	5
Horse	3	2
Goat	4	4
Monkey	4	3
Rooster	4	4
Dog	4	4
Pig	4	3

HORSE

	Business	Love
Rat	5	4
Ox	2	4
Tiger	1	2
Rabbit	2	2
Dragon	2	3
Snake	3	2
Horse	5	1
Goat	2	1
Monkey	4	5
Rooster	1	5
Dog	3	1
Pig	5	5

GOAT

	Business	Love
Rat	4	5
Ox	5	5
Tiger	4	3
Rabbit	2	2
Dragon	3	2
Snake	4	4
Horse	2	1
Goat	4	4
Monkey	3	3
Rooster	5	4
Dog	5	5
Pig	2	4

MONKEY

	Business	Love
Rat	3	2
Ox	5	3
Tiger	4	4
Rabbit	5	3
Dragon	1	1
Snake	4	3
Horse	4	5
Goat	3	3
Monkey	4	1
Rooster	5	4
Dog	5	3
Pig	1	2

ROOSTER

	Business	Love
Rat	5	5
Ox	3	2
Tiger	5	4
Rabbit	4	5
Dragon	1	3
Snake	4	4
Horse	1	5
Goat	5	5
Monkey	5	4
Rooster	5	4
Dog	5	4
Pig	4	3

ᴆOG

	Business	Love
Rat	4	3
Ox	5	3
Tiger	5	4
Rabbit	3	4
Dragon	5	5
Snake	4	4
Horse	3	1
Goat	5	5
Monkey	5	3
Rooster	5	4
Dog	4	3
Pig	2	1

ᴘIG

	Business	Love
Rat	3	3
Ox	2	2
Tiger	3	3
Rabbit	2	3
Dragon	1	4
Snake	4	3
Horse	5	5
Goat	2	4
Monkey	1	2
Rooster	4	3
Dog	2	1
Pig	2	1

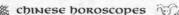 

We have now covered all the compatibilities and have covered all we set out to deal with in this book. Now, before finishing, you need to test yourself on this final chapter.

PRACTICE

We complete the book with a final test of your knowledge.

● You and your friend are both dragons. Do you work well in business together or in love, or neither?

● Your friend is a monkey. He asks you to think about going into business with him. You are a tiger. What advice does Chinese astrology give?

● Would a tiger be better off marrying a dragon or an ox?

● Would two snakes make good business partners?

I do hope that you have managed to learn something from the information given, which only really scratches the surface of Chinese horoscopes, and that you will utilise it to the best of your ability both in understanding yourself and in your dealings with your friends and family. I am a big advocate of getting to know and love yourself before getting to know and love other people, and I sincerely hope that the information given here will be of use and service to you, enabling you to reach that ultimate goal – a happy and loving life.

fURThER READING

Kristyna Arcarti, *I Ching for Beginners* (Headway, 1994)
Catherine Aubier, *Chinese Zodiac Signs* (Arrow, 1984)
Richard Craze, *Feng Shui for Beginners* (Headway, 1994)
Paula Delsol, *Chinese Horoscopes* (Pan, 1973)
Barry Fantoni, *Chinese Horoscopes* (Sphere, 1985)
Kwan Lau, *Secrets of Chinese Astrology* (Tengu Books, 1994)
Theodora Lau, *The Handbook of Chinese Horoscopes* (Arrow, 1981)
Neil Somerville, *Chinese Love Signs* (Thorsons, 1995)
Derek Walters, *Chinese Astrology* (Aquarian Press,1987)
Suzanne White, *The New Chinese Astrology* (Macmillan, 1993)